SCARS
of
1947

ADVANCE PRAISE FOR THE BOOK

'A balanced read with stories and facts that highlight an important aspect of our history. The book underscores the need for and importance of peace and love in the world we live in.'

—Shah Rukh Khan

'It is essential for stories of love and friendship to be told in order to remind the world of its own humanity. Especially at times like the ones we live in, the simplicity of Rajeev Shukla's writing is refreshing.'

—Priyanka Gandhi Vadra

'I found the book to have a great perspective on partition in terms of facts, stories and human resilience. It ushered memories of our cricket journey and the love we received from the people across the borders.'

—Sourav Ganguly

'In *Scars of 1947*, Rajeev Shukla compiles a series of fascinating, insightful personal stories of those affected by Partition. The traumatic foundational event of modern India can seem a historical abstraction to those who are generations removed from it, but Shukla's sensitively told tales bring life to the heartbreak, struggle, and (sometimes) reconciliation that followed. An important collection that revives stories that have gone untold for too long.'

—Shashi Tharoor

'The stories in the book take us through a journey of the tragic times Partition brought upon the people. My visit to Pakistan during the March series and time spent there will always hold a special place in my heart.'

—Suniel Shetty

'Bouncing back from adversity has always been the distinguishing character of humanity, and the book showcases that with the beautifully weaved real-life stories.'

—Sanjay Dutt

SCARS
of
1947
Real Partition Stories

RAJEEV SHUKLA

PENGUIN
VIKING
An imprint of Penguin Random House

VIKING

USA | Canada | UK | Ireland | Australia
New Zealand | India | South Africa | China

Viking is part of the Penguin Random House group of companies
whose addresses can be found at global.penguinrandomhouse.com

Published by Penguin Random House India Pvt. Ltd
4th Floor, Capital Tower 1, MG Road,
Gurugram 122 002, Haryana, India

Penguin
Random House
India

First published in Viking by Penguin Random House India 2022

ISBN 9780670095674

Typeset in Adobe Caslon Pro by Manipal Technologies Limited, Manipal
Printed at Replika Press Pvt. Ltd, India

www.penguin.co.in

MIX
Paper from
responsible sources
FSC® C016779

Contents

Prologue

The tragic Partition of India will never be forgotten by the people of the two countries that came into being after this event. A wound so deep, it has been and always will be passed on in the form of stories from one generation to the next—how, on the one hand, friends quickly turned foes and, on the other, help came from the most unexpected people. Those who witnessed and lived through those harrowing times proved to be far more than ordinary; their grit and determination to bury the tragic sight of their near and dear ones being killed in front of them and moving on to build a life from scratch are inspiring. As per official records, 1.2 million people were killed; violence erupted from the communal disharmony created by the sudden announcement of the mass relocation of people from one side of the border to the other.

During the creation of India and Pakistan, it is estimated that about 14 million people were uprooted and forced to leave everything behind to move to another country based on their religion. People were separated from their families and friends. The atmosphere was such that people had to leave their homes within a few hours as angry mobs targeted, attacked and killed families of other religions.

The people who were on the 'wrong' side of the border as per the new religious identities of these countries could not fathom how they were supposed to leave their ancestral homes, some that had been built hundreds of years before. The journeys were not planned, there was no systematic mode of transport and for a majority of the people walking was the only means by which to reach their unknown destinations, with a hope to live peacefully. Many had old parents who could not undertake this journey; children did not know whether to accept blessings and leave or stay back and be massacred by bloodthirsty mobs.

The prime objective of their journey was to stay alive; everything else had to be figured out along the way: their mode of transportation, food, safety measures, destinations, livelihoods and how they would care of their families.

The story was the same on either side of a hastily created border by the British. Hundreds of thousands of Hindus, Muslims and Sikhs lost their lives in this mass migration. People from both countries who lived through Partition and its aftermath have only one hope for generations to come: that such an event never take place again anywhere in the world; that people resolve their differences and not live with so much pain.

Authors from both sides of the border have written many books to voice their views on Partition, but few have showcased the real tragedy and pain that Partition caused. Over the course of the last three decades, I have met several people who were witnesses to this historic event and have carried in their hearts the excruciating pain caused by it. To get their first-hand accounts, I visited Pakistan over twenty times. In India, I interacted with people who were left with deep physical and emotional scars from the unfortunate incident.

The southern states of India were not as affected by the horrors as those belonging to Punjab or Bengal. Similarly, some places in Pakistan were also less affected. Partition heavily affected northern and eastern India and the Punjab and Sindh areas of Pakistan.

The stories in the book—of willpower, resilience and overcoming difficulties—are now more important than ever, given the global pandemic and disruption we are living through. In this book, you will find well-known names, but their stories were sadly unknown. Most names in the book are real, except a few that have been changed by their families to respect their privacy.

1

The Religion of Cricket

Taimur Bande

Taimur Bande, a citizen of Pakistan, resides in a cantonment area in Lahore. His paternal uncle was once elected as a member of the National Assembly from Lahore constituency. Taimur is a true nationalist devoted to the progress and development of his motherland. His love for Pakistan is such that any compliment to his country makes him glow with happiness. He is currently a professor of economics at a college situated in Lahore. Cricket is one of his passions and he cannot stand the defeat of the team representing his country. Taimur once visited India to cheer for Pakistan in the semi-final match of the World Cup series in Chandigarh. After the match, he was supposed to travel with me to Delhi, from where we were to fly to Mumbai to witness the glorious final match. Perhaps due to some technical fault in the Indian SIM card that he had been using, I could not get in touch with him after the match. I kept waiting for him at the Chandigarh airport for hours, but when he did not turn up, I decided to travel alone and reached Delhi late at night. Upon reaching, I established contact on the Pakistani SIM he had been carrying that seemed to be working. I asked him where he was, and the reply was quite a surprise to me. Despite the hotel rooms being booked and the flight from Delhi to Mumbai all set to take off on time, Taimur had gone back home to Lahore via the Wagah border from the Mohali stadium in Chandigarh itself—all because Pakistan had been defeated in the semi-finals!

Despite being a staunch nationalist, he never behaves or speaks in a manner that makes him sound anti-India. He loves India and pays equal respect to both countries and their people. Most of his friends are Indian and Hindu, and many are based in Gurugram in the National Capital Region. He has stayed for months at his friend's residence in Gurugram when he visited India. In addition to this, his friends from India also stay at his house in Lahore and address Taimur's mother as 'Ammi'. The warmth that exists among them is quite evident from the kind of support extended to Taimur's family when his Abba, Khalid Bande, was unfortunately murdered by some thieves. None of his relatives helped him during this troubled phase of his life when he needed them the most. However, Taimur's friends from India and their wives spent around a month at his place in Lahore and supported the family in that emotionally challenging time following the gruesome incident.

Born into a very well-to-do family, Taimur completed his education from universities abroad and also travels all over the world. He owns a beautiful bungalow in Lahore. In 1998, we got acquainted on a flight from Delhi to Lahore. I was on my way to Islamabad via Lahore while Taimur's destination was Lahore itself. I was supposed to interview some of the well-known personalities of Pakistan for my show *Ru-Ba-Ru*, which aired in the 1990s to early 2000s on the Zee channel. In those days, Taimur, then a lecturer at Lahore School of Law, used to go to Bangalore with the students for debate competitions; his students would win against their opponents most of the time. All those students belonged to affluent families and with their impressive command over the English language they got the better of their competitors in the debates. On the flight, Taimur and I quickly became friends. We started talking to each other over the phone later and met often. I felt we were so alike—our taste in food, our style of dressing, our dialects—everything was similar and it felt like we were just divided by the border. Whenever I visited his place, his mother would treat us with such affection that we felt like members of her own family. She would cook and serve us a spread of delicacies every time we visited. During those days, there was pressure building up to organize a cricket series between India and Pakistan. The Pakistan Cricket Board was insisting that the Indian cricket team visit Pakistan for a series as in those days, the Pakistan Cricket Board always supported the Board of Cricket Council in India (BCCI) in International Cricket Council (ICC) matters. Jagmohan Dalmia, the then head of the BCCI, also wanted the Indian cricket team to visit Pakistan for a series. Meanwhile, the Ministry of Home Affairs in India was not in favour of the idea. Apprehensive about the safety of the players following the terrorist attack on President Musharraf's convoy in Pakistan, the ministry decided to intervene. At this time the Indian cricket team was on a tour of Australia. I would receive phone calls from many senior players requesting to cancel the Pakistan tour since their family members were worried for their safety. Our players clearly and justifiably pointed out that if there were loopholes in the security of General Musharraf, then it was very hard to rely on any other type of security. BCCI head Jagmohan Dalmia was quite upset about this incident but was not ready to back out of the series. He appointed me to get permission from the government for this series, keeping in mind the fact that the minister of home affairs, L.K. Advani, was not in favour of giving his consent. Atal Bihari Vajpayee was serving as the head of the government then, with whom I was on good terms. I spoke directly to him and provided my point of view. I told him that there was a possibility that the series would help to reduce tension and build a strong relationship between the two nations. Vajpayee always dreamt of positive relations between India and Pakistan. With the support extended by Cabinet Minister Arun Jaitley, Foreign Affairs Minister Yashwant Sinha, along with the Principal Secretary to the Prime Minister Brajesh Mishra, I succeeded in convincing him. Sometime before that, I met President General Pervez Musharraf in Islamabad, who assured me that he would provide security equivalent to that of a president to the Indian cricket team. He said he would also reach out to the supporters of the Pakistani cricket team in the stadium and urge them to cheer for and welcome the Indian team with open arms.

The preparations for the India–Pakistan cricket series were in full swing. Dalmia monitored the progress daily. The Indian cricket team flew down to Delhi. Stalwarts like Sourav Ganguly, Sachin Tendulkar, Rahul Dravid and Anil Kumble were part of the team for the series. On the eve of their departure to Pakistan, I organized a meeting of home ministry officials with the entire cricket team at Taj Mansingh Hotel in Delhi to brief and reassure them about the security arrangements being adopted in Pakistan. The assurance that the team would be provided with adequate security was the first point in the meeting. The players were asked not to worry about their safety as it would be taken care of by the Pakistani government itself. Before flying to Pakistan, all the players were invited for tea at the prime minister's residence, where Vajpayee told Sourav Ganguly, the then team captain, that his wish was to win the hearts of the Pakistani people and not only the matches through this tournament. Initially, it was speculated that Prime Minister Vajpayee would himself visit Pakistan to attend a match. But later, Arun Jaitley came to Karachi instead. The prime minister's principal secretary, Brajesh Mishra, along with Vajpayee's son-in-law, Ranjan Bhattacharya, flew to Lahore as guests for another match.

One fine day, I got an unexpected call from Priyanka Gandhi Vadra (daughter of Rajiv Gandhi and granddaughter of Indira

Gandhi) that she, along with her brother Rahul Gandhi, would like to join us for a match in Karachi. I immediately informed the Pakistan Cricket Board about their arrival. The very next day, I received a message from Pakistan's prime minister, Zafarullah Khan Jamali, which stated that high-level security would be arranged for the members of the Gandhi family. A Pakistan Airlines aircraft equipped with first-class cabins was made to fly the Mumbai–Karachi route to bring over the Gandhis.

When Rahul, Priyanka and her husband, Robert Vadra, along with my wife, Anuradha, and I landed at Karachi airport, we were very surprised to see the extensive security arrangements in place. People had gathered in large numbers outside the airport in Karachi just to get a glimpse of the members of the Gandhi family. Shahryar Khan, who was serving as the chairman of the host cricket board, was present with his wife to receive us at the airport. To my amazement, the flow of traffic was blocked on the road to ensure smooth movement of all the vehicles in our convoy. Arrangements for our stay had been made at one of Karachi's exclusive government guest houses that once used to be the residence of the former prime minister Liaquat Ali Khan. The guest house was meant to accommodate the top brass of the government like the president or the prime minister.

The match being played in Karachi turned out to be a typical suspense-thriller India–Pakistan match; everyone was stressed about the outcome. There was nail-biting excitement. Amidst this highly stressful situation, the Karachi police commissioner came to our box at the stadium and warned us about the possibility of some violence on the roads if the results spelt a loss for Pakistan. As a safety measure, he advised the immediate departure of the Gandhis and requested them to go back to the guest house. Priyanka opposed it. She along with Jaitley refused to go anywhere before the match was over. Ashish Nehra bowled the last over that resulted in India's historic win in the match. Both Priyanka and Jaitley stood up in excitement and began to clap for India.

All cameras turned their focus on the cheerful Priyanka as she came out of the VIP box and started celebrating in the general public stands. When Priyanka and Rahul wanted to meet the teams after the match, I conveyed the request to Sourav Ganguly. He immediately asked the teams to get dressed and both the teams clicked memorable photographs with them. To our amazement, on our way back to the guest house, rather than any sort of violence, people were waving at us happily and warmly.

Another match was scheduled to be played in Lahore in a few days. I was all set to attend it. Gautam Singhania, the chairman and managing director of the Raymond Group, and Bollywood actor Suniel Shetty also joined us. The Indian audience in the stadium was warmly welcomed by the Pakistani nationals. Taxi drivers refused to charge fares from Team India supporters; shopkeepers were giving items to them free of cost. Such gestures were not even remotely imaginable till this time. The environment in both the countries was filled with warmth. In the box with us was Dina Wadia, the daughter of Pakistan's Quaid-e-Azam ('Great Leader'), Muhammad Ali Jinnah. She was accompanied by her son, Nusli Wadia, and grandsons, Ness and Jahangir. The entire country was in awe of her and her uncanny resemblance to her father. This was her first visit after her father's death in 1948 when she had come to pay her last tribute to the Quaid-e-Azam and had visited Jinnah's mausoleum 'Mazar-e-Quaid', his final resting place, in Karachi. The visit of Quaid-e-Azam's daughter was widely covered by the media across the country and became a historic event; it was a moment of great joy for everyone in Pakistan.

The positive energy and support among the spectators of the matches showed that General Musharraf had succeeded in keeping his promise. Every boundary hit by an Indian batsman drew cheers from the whole crowd. We were warmly welcomed by a band upon reaching the hotel Pearl Continental, where our team was staying. The players such as Tendulkar, Ganguly and Dravid met me every day and seemed happy. There was no fear of security lapses in their minds. They said they were not facing any problems or inconveniences and were glad the series had worked out. This series ended up playing a vital role in bridging the gap between the two nations.

A Handful of Bombay Soil

It was during this tour that I told Suniel Shetty about Taimur, my dear friend who had invited me for lunch to his place. I asked Shetty to accompany me and he graciously agreed. The people of Pakistan are diehard fans of Bollywood celebrities. In spite of any diplomatic tensions that may prevail between the two countries, Pakistanis love Bollywood films, songs and also TV soaps; these are an indispensable part of a majority of households in the country. We were enjoying the lunch at Taimur's residence in Lahore and admiring the beauty of his bungalow when I stumbled upon a room where I saw an aged, fair-complexioned and pretty woman who must have been in her eighties. She, very quietly, asked me to come inside and in Parsi-accented Marathi, which is common in Mumbai even today, curiously enquired, 'Are you from India?' When I answered in the affirmative, she said she had a favour to ask of me and requested me not to disclose it to any of her family members. She said, 'The moment I came to know about your visit to Lahore, I was eagerly waiting to meet you.' She asked when I was planning to visit Lahore again. I told her I was not sure and may visit in a few months. I asked her what I could do for her. I was very curious to know the reason she was asking such questions. She looked around to make sure no one was listening to our conversation and then said, 'I would like you to get me a handful of soil from Bombay.' She wanted to kiss the soil before leaving for her heavenly abode. I was confused and wondered why. Then she told me she was Taimur's maternal grandmother. 'Sixty years ago I came to Pakistan before Partition. Ever since then, I have not been able to visit Bombay. Now, all I am left with are the memories of my city for which my heart has always ached. Despite being a Pakistani by nationality, I still cannot tolerate it when anyone says anything offensive about India. I wanted to go to Bombay at least once before I breathed my last, but it seems difficult now. So, I want to at least rub the soil on my forehead and feel closer to India', she explained as tears rolled down my eyes listening to her.

I came out of the room and went to have my meal with the rest of the family in the dining room. Very quietly, I enquired from Taimur's mother, Zakiya, about the woman I met in the room. She was astounded. She said, 'Oh! So you met my mother!' She went on to tell me more about her history. 'My father, Mohammad Asgar Khan, served as an officer in the Indian Navy in Bombay before Partition. It was his first posting.' She said that they were Pathans from Peshawar. Her father was a very young and handsome man. He met a beautiful Parsi girl named Minni Chowksi, who was the daughter of a well-known freedom fighter and a senior leader in the Congress party in India. Chowksi's family had close ties with Mahatma Gandhi. Khan and Minni Chowksi fell for each other, and their love and affection made her go against the wishes of her family and she married Khan, moving to Peshawar with him. Minni Chowksi belonged to a rich and traditional Parsi family of Bombay and Asgar Khan belonged to a typical Pathan household. Minni adopted the Pathan culture where the burka became a part of her daily life. But she adopted the new Pathani traditions well. Since Taimur's mother, Zakiya, was Minni's only child, she brought along her mother after her father's demise to her marital house and ever since, Minni had become an integral part of the family. Taimur's entire family treated Minni with great love and respect. Despite being in Pakistan for almost six decades, Minni still harboured deep love for India in her heart. She adored everything about India. The medicines prescribed to her were all imported from India. No one in the family dared to express any anti-India sentiments in front of her; during every cricket match between the two countries, while every member of the house cheered for Pakistan, Minni cheered for India. If India won, she felt happy but if they lost the match, she would not eat anything for dinner. Her family, especially Taimur, loved her fervour for India.

After listening to Zakiya, the entire matter became clear as day to me. However, I preferred not to talk about Minni's request for Indian soil. I shared the conversation only with Suniel Shetty. He too got very emotional. Both of us went to Minni's room and brought her out in a wheelchair to the living room. Shetty spoke to her in Marathi. As soon as he started talking to her in Marathi, she was ecstatic and said that she was speaking her mother tongue after almost sixty long years. She spoke in Marathi for a long time and her face glowed with happiness. The other members of the family were astonished hearing her fluent Marathi. Before coming to Pakistan, Suniel had brought a small flag of India to cheer for the team during the cricket match. Looking at the intensity of her affection towards India, he gifted this flag to Minni. After a few years, Taimur often laughingly used to mention that his Naani (maternal grandmother) would sit in her wheelchair in front of the television for every India–Pakistan match holding the same Indian flag to cheer for India.

After coming back to India from Lahore, I got in touch with the officers of the Ministry of External Affairs to get Minni a visa and arranged for her to visit Mumbai. But, due to her deteriorating health, she could not visit despite wanting to as much as she did. Moreover, I could also not get her the soil she had asked for, but I would send her gifts which made her very happy and she would thank me for them. She once said to me, 'Oh beta! I have no words to thank you. Though you could not get me the soil I had asked for, the Indian flag was a priceless gift and I feel connected to my motherland even though I reside in Pakistan. I now kiss the flag often and will be able to depart for my final journey in peace.' After around eight years, she passed away at the age of eighty-eight, leaving behind memories that anyone who knew her would never forget. Even today, her face and words resonate in my heart and mind.

From Kasauli to Lahore

Taimur Bande's family had a strange connection with India. I once visited Taimur's Daadi (paternal grandmother), Raahat Bande, during one of my trips to Lahore. She used to stay with Taimur's paternal uncle. She belonged to Kasauli, a beautiful hill station located in the Indian state of Himachal Pradesh. She was forced to leave her home overnight with her husband and son, Khalid (Taimur's father), who was hardly a year old at the time of Partition. Narrating her past, she said that they owned a beautiful house in Kasauli and were quite well-off. She had a luxurious, comfortable and enjoyable life there. Raahat described how people from different religious backgrounds, especially Hindus and Muslims, lived together like family. Everyone would watch folk performances of the Ramlila together. There was a temple that they used to visit to have prasad, which she would touch to her forehead before eating. Muslims used to enjoy Holi and Diwali with the same spirit and enthusiasm as they would any of their own religious festivals. She used to sing bhajans in that temple too, she remembers. Kasauli was considered a safe place even during the worsening atmosphere of Partition. A few people they knew from Amritsar and Punjab had come to her house in Kasauli to seek shelter from the riots.

Kasauli, Dalhousie and Shimla were the preferred summer destinations for the rich families of Lahore. Many of them had bought vacation homes in Kasauli and Shimla, where they used to spend their summers. Taimur's grandmother said that things were going very well and people were living peacefully for a long time. Almost all the friends of her husband, Khwaja Badruddin Bande, were Hindus. Aloo parathas were something he would die for. One fine day, Raahat made him parathas for dinner. While he was enjoying the meal with the three vegetable dishes that she had made, one of their Hindu friends barged into their house suddenly and advised them to leave for Pakistan that very night. This left them completely shocked. The chaos, extreme violence and aggression that had erupted among the Sikhs of Punjab was making its way to Kasauli, it seemed. The family hurriedly began packing their clothes, jewellery, etc., but Raahat said she could not pack anything to eat. Her husband did not let her waste any more time. With just a few clothes and Badruddin's favourite fur coat and a few carpets, they were all set to bid goodbye to their abode forever. The Hindu friends of Badruddin managed to arrange for a vehicle and a Hindu driver to drop them off safely to a cantonment in Ambala. Their Hindu friend got in touch with someone influential and got them accommodation at the cantonment itself with the army officers. People were being sent to different places from there under the supervision of the army officers. Their family stayed in the camp for three days and was provided with a bag full of rice that they used to eat after sprinkling some salt and chillies on it. Upon their turn after three days, they were sent to Lahore in a truck. No food was loaded onto the truck but they had taken along an earthen pot filled with water. They were accompanied by a British officer on a motorcycle who was guiding the truck. While approaching Ludhiana, the truck ran out of fuel, and unfortunately, no one at the petrol pumps were ready to refill the truck since they were heading towards Pakistan. Nobody was paying any heed to the British officer either. A kind-hearted Sikh man, who was a fuel dealer, agreed to provide fuel for their truck. Somehow, they were able to cross Ludhiana. They saw many disturbing sights along the way like dead bodies lying on the roads with stray dogs feeding on them. They were horrified to see dead bodies of young children. Hindus, Muslims and Sikhs all seemed to have been killed. The situation was such that everyone was heinously killing each other. Slowly, dodging the bodies, the truck headed towards Amritsar.

Because Raahat had not eaten anything, she was unable to breastfeed her one-year-old son, Khalid, who was continuously crying out of hunger. A Muslim man who was sitting right in front of her whom they had befriended earlier never offered to share his food even though her son kept crying. Finally, she begged for two semolina dates from Murtaja, an army officer who was travelling in the truck with them. He gave them to her and thereafter, she could finally breastfeed her son. When they reached Amritsar, she, along with some other ladies, requested the driver to stop the truck so that they could relieve themselves. Amritsar was witnessing terrible riots. Houses were set on fire and some Sikh men were standing on the roofs of their houses with big rifles and swords. While on their way back to the truck after the toilet break, she encountered a Sikh man who pointed a rifle at her chest. She said she felt a shiver down her spine thinking it was the end of her life. She was holding her son in her arms. For a few seconds, the Sikh man kept staring at her and then it seemed that something struck him and he said, 'Sister . . . you may go . . . I will not kill you, but do remember how people from your community killed my wife and children.' Raahat said her eyes filled with tears as she returned to the truck.

I asked Raahat Bande about the British officer who was leading the truck, whether he stepped forward to protect her or not. She said the officer was looking after the safety of the truck. He was all alone and was very scared for his life seeing the violence caused by the rioters. She said things would turn ugly based on mere rumours. Muslims were being instigated by other Muslims against the Hindus and the Sikhs; they were told that Hindus and Sikhs were killing Muslims travelling by trains and the Hindus and Sikhs were told that Muslims were killing their people. But the rumours were spread in such a convincing and provoking manner that people became hot under the collar. They were being instigated and brainwashed against one another in such a way that they never gave it a second thought before killing others. Aggression and the desire to take revenge overpowered the need to know the truth.

I saw the tears roll down her cheeks as she was narrating her sad past. She told me that they reached Lahore in the evening somehow with their body and soul together. She was utterly exhausted and had fallen asleep in the truck. Suddenly she woke up startled when she heard the loud chanting of slogans like 'Long Live Pakistan!', 'Long Live Madr-e-Millat Fatima', 'Long Live Quaid-e-Azam!' Raahat and her family were ecstatic. Upon disembarking from the truck, they were served chana pulao. The truck driver dropped them off at Lahore Cantonment. They were not afraid of losing their lives anymore. There was a residential area nearby on McLeod Road, where many houses had been abandoned by the Hindus and Sikhs. They settled in one of them. The house had a lot of tin boxes filled with mustard oil, pure ghee and some flour and rice. That house belonged to a Lalaji, who had abandoned it the previous night and left for India in the same way they were forced to leave their house in India. She told me, 'I cooked some rice and offered it to my husband with some ghee from the tin box. The moment I offered that food to him, he asked me where the food had come from. I replied that it belonged to those who used to reside in the house. He refused to eat the food saying he could feel the pain of the owners of the house who had to leave everything they owned. He said their pain and suffering perfectly replicated his own. He said that at the end of the day they were all humans and that how senseless it was that their religious interests had turned them into enemies overnight. He asked me to imagine how I would feel if some strangers were to eat the parathas he left behind in Kasauli.' He firmly refused to use any of that person's belongings and decided to get some flour and pulses from a nearby store and that was finally what the family ate.

Taimur's grandfather was very particular when it came to his ideology and morals. He was emotional and kind-hearted. He was very attached to his friends from Kasauli, whom he could never forget till his last breath. He felt that was a great loss for him and would cry when remembering them. During the 1965 Indo-Pak war, every other day they would hear announcements about the possibility of being bombed by the Indian Air Force, fearing which they would hide under the staircase of the house. But no one would utter anything against India. I was told by Raahat Bande that her husband kept reiterating that Partition only created a mess and that nothing changed for the good. He felt that people who killed innocent people would have to pay for their deeds. 'What was the need to divide people when they were living peacefully? How did it change anyone's life for the better?' No one would argue with him then.

'Beta, even I feel the same way as him', said Raahat Bande. 'The day we reached Lahore, from the rooftop of our new house, I saw two Sikh men being chased by a Muslim mob. Those Muslim men mercilessly stabbed both the Sikhs.' Raahat yelled at the top of her voice asking them to stop, but she was reduced to being a helpless eyewitness to the brutal murders. 'That unfortunate scene flashes before my eyes even today. I was so pained by the incident that I couldn't eat anything for the next two days.' She could not control her tears while talking to me about the incident. I was moved to think that people are still living with these traumatic memories.

It was in 2013 that I met Raahat Bande and got to hear her story. Taimur's grandmother, even then, after sixty-six years, remembered and was deeply affected by what she saw from the terrace that day. People like her not only witnessed the murders but unfortunately carried the burden of their memories and trauma forever. There were thousands of cases in which Hindus and Sikhs together saved many Muslim lives and vice versa. Taimur's grandmother passed away a few years ago, leaving behind some unforgettable memories. The image of her sad face with tears rolling down her eyes is still fresh in my mind.

These two real-life incidents are from one family. The first one was linked to Taimur's maternal grandmother, Minni Chowksi, and the second to his paternal grandmother, Raahat Bande. This is probably the reason why Taimur, in spite of being a true Pakistani, does not harbour any hatred for Indians.

2

Babuji and His Jewels
Dr Arun Kumar and His Father Ramlal Kumar

When I used to stay at Asiad Village in New Delhi, Dr Arun Kumar was my neighbour. He specialized in paediatrics and was practising in a hospital located in Ghaziabad. His better half, Rani Kumar, was serving as a professor at All India Institute of Medical Sciences (AIIMS). My friends from Pakistan used to frequent my house in those days and Dr Kumar was well aware of it. He once told me that his Babuji, his father, wanted to meet me but I did not know the reason. Upon his request, I met his father after two days. The time of the meeting was planned by Babuji in such a way that both his son and daughter-in-law were at work at their respective hospitals.

At the age of eighty-five, in the year 2000, Ramlal Kumar used to go daily to work on his scooter to earn a salary of Rs 20,000. The day I met him, he had intentionally taken a day off from work and, over a cup of tea, he started talking to me and said, 'Beta, do you visit Pakistan frequently? I have watched your interviews with Nawaz Sharif and Benazir Bhutto; it seems that you are quite known among the political fraternity over there.' I said, 'Yes, Babuji, that is true.' He then said, 'I want you to do me a favour,' and requested me not to disclose it to his family members. I agreed to it. Thereafter, he went on to narrate the story about his days that were spent in Lahore:

'I was a very well-known and wealthy builder in Lahore. I had constructed a number of buildings and just about three months before the day that marked the beginning of Partition, I had purchased three bungalows in one of the posh localities of Lahore named Model Town. I used to earn Rs 5000 as rent from leased houses on a daily basis, which would be lakhs of rupees today. I had many shops and houses in my name. When the city began to witness riots, many people I knew left their homes permanently to settle in India, but I lived in a colony near Lahori Gate named "Chidhewali Gali" (Bird's Lane) with some of my relatives. The Muslim residents of that colony used to respect me a lot and I was assured of my well-being by them. When the violence was at its peak and the Pathans were also heading towards Lahore from Peshawar to commit heinous crimes like loot and murder, a Muslim man, who was my hairdresser, came to me one night and said, "Sahab, the situation in Lahore is deteriorating. The young boys of the colony are getting out of control and are conspiring to attack you. They have become pugnacious as a result of this widespread hatred towards other religious communities. Last night when you were returning from your office, one of the persons residing in this colony itself had planned to stab you with a dagger, but I somehow stopped him from doing so. I would suggest you leave from here for fifteen days till this matter gets back to normal."

Upon comprehending the situation, along with my wife, my one-year-old son (Dr Kumar) and rest of the kids, I left for Vrindavan. Since I was supposed to return after fifteen days, I had taken along just a few pairs of clothes and Rs 10,000. In the span of those few days, Partition was announced, and Lahore was declared a part of Pakistan. I had nothing except Rs 10,000 now with me and that too was being spent on our upkeep. All of a sudden my immense wealth and property in Lahore became non-existent. I travelled to Shimla with my family after spending fifteen days in Vrindavan and decided to spend a few days there. I was struggling to keep my mind off the memories of Lahore and decided to revisit the city as soon as I could to bring back my belongings. After a few days, I followed my instincts and finally made my way back to Lahore. I left my wife and children in Shimla and boarded a train from Kalka station to Lahore by myself. It was seven in the evening when I reached Lahore. I found it nearly impossible to escape the loneliness the city was engulfed in. The roads were deserted, there was not even a single vehicle in sight, riots were raging all over the city. I hired a tonga and continued nevertheless to make my way towards my home. The Muslim tonga-driver realized that I was a Hindu businessman and warned me about my safety, but at the same time, assured me that he would get me to my destination safely. He asked me to let him do the talking if someone stopped us, so he could convince them that I was a Muslim. I reached my locality and it was bustling with people. I covered my face with a towel and used the darkness to get to my house. I had left the house under the supervision of my servant Hafiz, who was guarding the house with absolute attentiveness. He informed me that mobs of looters came by a few times and enquired about my whereabouts. When he told them that I had left Lahore, they went away. They wanted to destroy and loot the property, but Hafiz, along with some of our neighbours, did not let them break in and stood firm, guarding my house while putting their own lives at risk. I quickly packed all of my belongings and stuffed them into two trunks. One of the trunks was packed with precious items like jewellery and cash, and another one had our clothes and other items. Meanwhile, I got to know that my brother-in-law, who was in Lahore, was leaving for India that night itself and had rented a truck for the journey. My elder sister was married to him and we had a good relationship. I thought that one of my trunks packed with money and jewellery would safely reach India in the truck that they had hired. I approached my brother-in-law that night and requested him to take along my trunk with him. Once that was done, I boarded a train from Lahore for Kalka at 4 a.m. with the other trunk that had the regular items. Before leaving for India, I had to come to terms with the fact that I was leaving Lahore forever. I, therefore, decided to hand over the documents of my house, plots, shops and other houses that I owned to my loyal servant, Hafiz, and drafted a legal document according to which Hafiz would be the beneficiary of all of my assets. When I returned to Shimla, I felt carefree knowing that whatever valuables I had brought from Lahore would help me lead a decent life.

On the third day of my return, I visited my brother-in-law's place to collect the trunk that I had given him. I was presented with great hospitality upon my visit, but when I got up to leave, my brother-in-law informed me that he had left my trunk in Lahore since he himself was carrying a lot of luggage with him and the truck driver was not ready to load more luggage in the truck as there was no space. All of a sudden I felt like the rug below my feet had been pulled away. I was shocked beyond belief. I felt numb for a moment and felt as if I would faint; whatever I thought I would use to begin my new life in India was all gone. I begged my brother-in-law over and over for the trunk but he firmly maintained that he left it in Lahore. I was aware of the fact that my brother-in-law was financially not very well off. I somehow consoled myself of the loss and returned home. For days, I could neither sleep nor eat any food after what seemed like my brother-in-law's sudden change of heart. I had a strong feeling that my belongings were siphoned off by my own relative. I got to know that my brother-in-law had purchased shops and houses after three months of moving to India and had started investing money in new businesses. I was betrayed indeed and became a victim of treachery. My brother-in-law's financial condition was not strong enough to buy those properties by himself. I was convinced that it was my hard-earned money with which my brother-in-law set up a new foundation for his own future. Unfortunately, I could not file a case in a court of law as I had no evidence against him.'

Shedding tears, Babuji continued to express his grief. He could not claim compensation that was being offered by the Indian government for the properties he owned and was forced to leave in Lahore since the documents of the properties—based on which people were getting property and compensation in India—had been handed over to his help, Hafiz, in Lahore.

I consoled him and, thereafter, he continued to narrate his sad past:

'I had no choice but to begin from scratch as my life had completely turned for the worse. I tried to make ends meet by engaging in work related to coal picking alongside a railway track in Shimla. Gradually, I got to work as a clerk in the accountant general's office and after my duty was over, I would sell hair combs on the road in the evening to ensure my survival. My father-in-law, Kishan Chandra Madaan, stayed with us. He was a well-known moneylender among the Britishers in Lahore. He would lend money to them on interest and also provide them with furniture and other essential goods which these officers needed to furnish their houses on being transferred to Lahore. The Britishers would return those goods to him. Kishan Chandra's business flourished and made him a millionaire. But his riches turned to rags as all of his assets and the money he had earned were left behind in Lahore. Now, I had to shoulder the responsibility of taking care of not only myself but my relatives as well.'

Babuji said that he had purchased three shops in Anarkali Bazaar in Lahore and each would earn him rent of Rs 250 every month. He had a bungalow on Nisbat Road and Lawrence Road. Besides that, he had given one bungalow on rent in Model Town and also had two plots there. But, in spite of having properties at these posh locations, Babuji used to live in his ancestral house in Chidhewali Gali near Lahori Gate. 'Chidhewala' was a very busy lane and he had three houses there. His father-in-law,

Kishan Chandra Madaan, resided in the same colony. Babuji talked about his brother-in-law, who found a runaway kid from Daska, Punjab, crying at the Lahore railway station and decided to bring him along to his shop; the boy's name was Raunaq Singh. He started working at their family-owned shop in Lahore and assisted in dealing with customers at the shop and taking care of their home. He was paid Rs 20 each month. His brother-in-law relied on Raunaq Singh for helping him out even in his new shop that dealt in steel pipes that he had set up in Hauz Qazi Delhi, after Partition. Gradually, Raunaq got involved in more and more dealings of their businesses and was often sent to Calcutta to look after business-related matters. With the passage of time, Raunaq became experienced enough to take the bold step of starting a business of his own. After getting permission from Ram Kumar's brother-in-law, Raunaq set up his own shop by selling his wife's jewellery for Rs 8000. He secured a contract to supply pipe railing for the grand Republic Day celebrations in Delhi. The boy who was once a helper later became a multimillionaire industrialist of India, Sardar Raunaq Singh, who owned big brands like Apollo Tyres and many other big companies. Back in those days in Lahore, when Raunaq worked for a petty amount as a helper in the shop, an astrologer, Pandit Roopchand, used to visit them. He once prepared Raunaq's horoscope to see what destiny had in store for him. Roopchand's prediction was correct in all aspects when he told Ram Kumar's brother-in-law that his helper would make millions in the future and would become very famous throughout the country, racing ahead of him. But no one believed in his prediction then.

Babuji further spoke about his father-in-law Kishan:

My father-in-law was involved in a land dispute with his sister. His case was being contested by Advocate Muhammad Ali Jinnah in the Bombay High Court. One day, he decided to meet Jinnah, who spent almost an hour and half chatting with him, talking about Lahore and other things. When Ram Kumar emerged out of Jinnah's room, he was handed over a bill by his secretary. Jinnah had charged him a fee on a minute basis, which he would do for every meeting. Thereafter, Ram Kumar did not even allow the thought of meeting Jinnah, except for discussing the important facts of his case.

Babuji said that his father-in-law, mother-in-law and sisters-in-law lived in a dharamshala in Vrindavan with their children right after Partition, but from there, he, along with his wife Roop Kumari and the children, travelled to Shimla and settled there. Later, he retired from the Ministry of Finance, Delhi. But Babuji's sister-in-law lived in Vrindavan for four years and became a devotee of Krishna. His mother-in-law died of shock upon learning about Partition. She used to say, '*Rani goli ho gayi, aur goli rani*', which means that the queen became the serving girl, and the serving girl became the queen (a reference from a popular story recited during the festival of Karva Chauth, where wives fast praying for their husband's long life).

One of his sisters-in-law, Kusumlata aka Bimla, was still residing in Delhi. When I met her, she confirmed every word of Babuji's story and spoke about the Thakardas settlement near Chidhewala Lane where many of her relatives used to reside.

Subsequently, I asked Babuji, 'Why did you want to meet me? What is it that you want?' He said, 'I want you to do me a favour. I have an important task for you. Actually, I had buried some precious jewels—gold, diamonds and silver—in huge quantities in the house I used to reside in Lahore, which today should be valued at not less than 200 crore rupees. Since I was in a hurry to leave that place following the riots, I could not bring those along. They have been buried under a thick wall beneath the ground and that wall is the foundation of the entire structure. Those jewels can be extracted only if the entire house is demolished. I want you to find out whether the old houses in that locality are still intact or have they been demolished and replaced with new construction.'

I agreed to help him and asked for the house number. He refused to share the house number and said that he would prefer not to tell me the exact address of the house because the moment anyone would come to know about the treasure, they might encroach or purchase the house to get hold of the treasure. Keeping that in mind, he said that he would give me a clue about the exact location of the house by giving details about the surrounding areas and requested me to meet the government officials in Lahore to negotiate the division of the treasure in such a way that Babuji gets fifty per cent of it and rest can be forfeited to the Pakistan government.

I knew that it was impossible to arrange such a deal. Even if the treasure was found, it would come under the Enemy Property Act, which states that the belongings of a native of the enemy state will be forfeited completely to the government—in this case, the government of Pakistan would become the owner of the forfeited properties. Under no circumstances could it be brought back to India, but, for Babuji's sake, I asked for the address of the locality where his house was located and gave him the assurance that I would find a way out. I got in touch with my friend Yawar over the phone, who resides in Lahore, to seek his help in this matter. I requested him to visit that place in Lahore and inform me about the present-day condition of that locality, whether the old houses were still intact or had the place been constructed over. However, I made sure not to divulge the real reason for the enquiry during our conversation. The very next day, over the phone, Yawar gave me an update. He told me that the locality was a residential area of old Lahore and was occupied by people from the lower middle classes. None of the houses had been renovated or reconstructed. Highlighting the extremely narrow and busy lanes of the area, he said it was nearly impossible to drive a car through them. When I informed Babuji about the same, he was in heaven and started seeing a ray of hope. He would ask me repeatedly to speak to some Pakistani government officials and crack a deal. I was very confused. I did not know how to tell Babuji that the hope of a deal was nothing but will-o'-the-wisp. Babuji was not ready to share the exact address of the house until the deal was finalized. When I felt it was high time, I decided to reveal the story of the treasure to Yawar. His father was serving as the chief secretary of Punjab (in Pakistan) and he simply denied any possibility of getting any part of the treasure back to India, stating that it now legally belonged to Pakistan, and even if the official orders of excavation were given and it was found, it would reach nowhere other than the Pakistan government's treasury. When I told this to Babuji, he became very upset. He was in despair, since the last hope of recovering the valuables that he had left behind in Lahore was lost. Thereafter, he didn't talk much with me in our subsequent meetings. Many a times, I even tried to ask for the exact address of that house with the hope that something could be done, but he simply refused. He never shared that address even with his son or daughter-in-law. He passed away a few years ago.

The story of Babuji's treasure ends on a sad note. But he was an eighty-five-year-old strong-willed personality who would go to his workplace on a two-wheeler. Every day he used to climb up and down the stairs of a four-storied building and was dedicated to remaining self-reliant till his last breath, even though his children took good care of him.

3

The Heerey and Kheerey of Model Town
Fakirchand Anand

I often wondered that had Babuji (Ramlal Kumar) shifted to the posh and safe locality of Model Town, where he owned houses, he would not have sealed his fate. Talking about Model Town, I would like to take a short detour before delving into the story of Fakirchand Anand.

Back in those days, Model Town was an upcoming posh locality of Lahore, whose residents were rich and highly educated. They were largely Hindus from the upper strata of society, who maintained very cordial relations with one another. Model Town still maintains its identity as one of the best residential areas of Lahore. Nawaz Sharif, the former prime minister of Pakistan, and Nusrat Fateh Ali Khan, the legendary singer, used to live there. I distinctly remember how well maintained the locality was when I once visited the place to interview Nusrat Fateh Ali Khan for my TV show *Ru-Ba-Ru*; the entire locality had an upper-class aura. While I was on my way to the ustad's house, there was a crossing near which I saw a two-storey building that was home to the famous singer Noor Jehan. Later, her daughter used to live in that house.

Noor Jehan was a close friend of Lata Mangeshkar (a renowned Indian singer) and they shared a mutual admiration for each other. Lataji herself told me that once they met at the Wagah border at the Border Security Force (BSF) guest house. Noor Jehan brought famous dishes from Lahore to the meeting while Mangeshkar treated her to Marathi food. The meeting was organized by the policemen and government officials from both sides of the border. Lata Mangeshkar was and continues to be a highly regarded and popular singer in Pakistan as well. Her songs are enjoyed by everyone there. I came to know about the extent of her popularity and massive fan following through a government official of Pakistan, who said that it would be next to impossible to control the crowd by simply deploying the police force if she were to perform in a live concert; they would definitely need to deploy the army to manage the crowd. He also mentioned how the people of Pakistan loved Jagjit Singh. He seems to enjoy a fan following that was as big if not bigger than their own famous ghazal singer Mehdi Hassan. However, talking about Lataji, he expressed his disappointment over the fact that she could never visit Pakistan. The great desire of the Pakistanis to see her perform live could not be fulfilled.

The strong bond and respect that existed between Mehdi Hassan and Lata Mangeshkar is known to only a few. Lataji told me an incident that took place on one of her visits to Ottawa in Canada. The day she reached, her host informed her of a show where Mehdi Hassan was performing. He asked her if she would like to attend it. She agreed and attended the show as a member of the audience, concealing her identity. While the whole audience was enjoying the show, Hassan suddenly spotted the legend in the audience. He paused in the middle of his performance and said, 'Such a great and talented personality is sitting amidst us; it won't be fair on my part to continue to sing.' He approached

Lataji and escorted her to the stage. When the audience, most of whom were Pakistani, came to know about her presence, they stood up and applauded her until she sat down. Hassan sought Lataji's permission before resuming his performance as a gesture of respect. They also performed a few songs together later.

Kapurthala–Lahore–Delhi

Let us come back to our narrative about Model Town. This story has its roots in one of my conversations with Som Anand, a famous writer from Lahore. The incident was later also confirmed by him in a chapter of the book *Lahore 1947*, compiled by Salim Ahmed, and is about his father, Fakirchand Anand, a famous banker who lived in posh Model Town. He had purchased a new bungalow there that he truly cherished. When most of the people were leaving Lahore as a result of the riots, Anand did not abandon his house, thinking it to be a temporary problem that would get resolved soon. While the entire city of Lahore was witnessing deadly attacks on the Hindus and Sikhs, Model Town turned out to be the safest place. There were many villages near Model Town like Jeun Hana, which were dominantly occupied by Gujjar Muslims, but not a single villager would go to Model Town with the intention of creating any violence. As a matter of fact, many of the villagers used to deliver milk and vegetables to the doorstep of Model Town residents and came forward to protect the Hindu and Sikh residents of the area against the rioters without sparing a thought. The riots in other areas of the city had almost no impact on Model Town. Even during the time when the violence was at its peak, Anand travelled to meet his best friend Aziz Baksh in Kapurthala (Punjab, India) in his limousine. When Anand was set to return to his home in Lahore, Aziz's family requested him not to go back as people had become violent and were on a bloodthirsty rampage along the way back to his home. However, Anand was so attached to his

city, and especially to his home in Model Town, that he turned
a deaf ear to all their appeals.

Gulzara Singh, Anand's driver, was a very faithful and obedient
person. He was the one who drove him to Kapurthala, despite
the great risk, encountering innumerable dead bodies on the way.
People from neither the Sikh nor the Muslim communities were
sparing a single chance to kill each other. But Anand had made
up his mind about his return; he was stubborn and wanted to go
back to Lahore. To assuage him, Gulzara Singh untied his turban
and placed it at Anand's feet, and said, 'You may shoot me right
away if you want, but I will not go back to Lahore.' Consequently,
Anand decided to leave Gulzara there and Aziz Baksh's cousin
brother drove him back to his home. It was decided that till the
Wagah border, Aziz's cousin would wear a Gandhi cap which was
a white khadi sidecap, pointed in the front and back and with a
wide band. And the moment he would enter Pakistani territory,
he would replace it with a Jinnah cap, which was a fur qaraqul
hat named after the founder of Pakistan, Muhammad Ali Jinnah.
The cap was worn by many early politicians of Pakistan, especially
those from the founding party: the Pakistan Muslim League. This
ploy helped them reach Lahore safely.

Anand had a neighbour who was a maulvi. His name was
Mohammad Ahmad. He was a devoted follower of Mahatma
Gandhi and the Congress's principles, but anti-Jinnah. However,
his better half was just the opposite in this regard. She was a
supporter of Jinnah's ideology. Both of them often got into
arguments and quarrels due to this difference in opinion. When
Gandhi and Nehru urged people to celebrate the independence of
the nation that was about to be declared by hoisting the tricolour
flag in their homes, Jinnah asked people to oppose Gandhi's
proposal because, according to him, true independence would
come only if Pakistan was brought into existence. Maulvi Sahab
celebrated the moment by hoisting the tricolour Indian flag, but
his begum sahiba instead waved a black flag from the roof of their

house. Although Maulvi Sahab's wife was not a highly educated person, her brothers were well-known Urdu authors, editors and poets. One of her brothers, named Raja Mehdi Ali Khan, decided to settle in Bombay in India, instead of Pakistan. He became a famous lyricist in Bollywood and worked very closely with music directors like Madan Mohan. *'Naino mein badra chhaye'* (from the film *Mera Saya*), *'Lag ja galey'* (*Woh Kaun Thi*), *'Jhumka gira re bareilli ke bazaar mein'* (*Mera Saya*), *'Mera sundar sapna toot gaya'* (*Do Bhai*), *'Watan ki raah mein watan ke naujawan shaheed hon'* (*Shaheed*), *'Main pyaar ka raahee hoon'* (*Ek Musafir Ek Hasoona*), etc. are some of his works.

Raja Mehdi Ali Khan lived in the Jhelum district of Pakistan but decided to spend the rest of his life in India. He composed many patriotic songs and also worked with the All India Radio. He had got a chance to work with the eminent writer Saadat Hasan Manto, and it was he who referred Raja Mehdi Ali to famous Indian film actor Ashok Kumar, so that he could exhibit his talent in films as well.

Fakirchand Anand's son, Som Anand, who later became a known Urdu author and journalist, would visit his neighbour Maulvi Mohammad Ahmad's house to learn Urdu from his wife, who treated him like her own son. Meanwhile, Lahore continued to burn with incessant riots for a very long time. Standing on the roof of his house, Anand would watch the aftermath of the riots and the violence, rising up in the sky in the form of dark clouds of smoke indicating the loss of innumerable lives and properties. The areas and localities that were set ablaze included Shah Alami, Lakshmi Chowk, Anarkali, Gwalmandi, Taksaal Gali, Lahori Gate, Copper Road and Beadon Road. Most of the Sikhs and Hindus had left Model Town with their belongings by that time, but Anand stayed on with the same poise. He was just not ready to leave.

The point I want to highlight is that all the Hindus and Sikhs who lived in the Model Town area were not *forced* to leave all of a sudden. They had the chance to travel to India and settle there in a well-organized manner. They properly packed their belongings like money, clothes, jewellery, etc. and left for India in trucks that were guarded by army soldiers. Except their houses, nothing was left behind. Babuji, Ramlal Kumar, whose story we read in the previous chapter, had purchased three plots and a house in Model Town, and quite possibly, he would not have had to go through so much pain and regret all through the remainder of his life in India had he managed to shift to Model Town. If Babuji had the opportunity to bring all of his valuable belongings like money and jewellery to India, the trauma that Partition forced upon him may have been eased a bit. But I imagine he did not want to leave the ancestral home in Chidhewali Gali because of all the treasure he had hidden beneath a thick wall of the house.

Meanwhile Anand started receiving frantic calls for help through letters from his best friend Aziz Baksh in Kapurthala. Muslims were being killed every day and all of them had left Kapurthala. There was so much violence on the roads that no one knew how many of them had been able to complete their journeys safely. And now Aziz Baksh was getting very worried about his own safety. Anand decided to leave for Kapurthala to save his friend's life. His family members warned him that it was not safe at all for him to step out of the house. But Anand did not pay any attention to them and said, 'I don't care about my life, but I will do my best to save my friend.'

Anand also came to know of an incident in which Muslims travelling from Punjab to Lahore by train were massacred on a railway bridge near Kapurthala a few days back. Anand feared that Aziz and his family might have boarded the same train. He quickly got in touch with one of his Sikh friends, B.B.S. Bedi, who was a leader of the communist party, and they left for Kapurthala to look for Aziz and his family. With great difficulty, they both somehow reached Kapurthala and found that Aziz and his family had not embarked on the ill-fated train journey and were alive.

On their way back to Lahore with Aziz and family, their vehicle was stopped by a group of young Sikh men who asked them to hand over all the Muslim passengers. There was not a single police officer present and Anand was frightened. Bedi, however, managed to get everyone out of the dangerous situation. He not only convinced the angry Sikh men to let them go, but also gave a passionate speech like a typical politician. Influenced by this, the group decided to spare them. Now, they all were heading towards Lahore in Anand's limousine. By late evening, they finally reached Anand's house in Model Town.

Aziz Baksh and his whole family were now living at Anand's house. It bustled with people. One day Anand had gone out with his friend Bedi for a meeting in Lahore city, and Anand's son Som had gone to meet his neighbour. Aziz Baksh and Anand's families were still in the house. Suddenly, the house was attacked by Pathans. Seeing this, their neighbour Maulvi Sahab came out of his house and engaged the mob in conversation. In the meanwhile, the maulvi's wife very cleverly helped the family escape from the back door and brought them to her house safely. Aziz's wife refused to leave the house thinking that the Pathans would spare her as she was Muslim. But the mob vandalized Anand's home and started beating Aziz's wife. She pleaded with them and told them she was Muslim, but the Pathans said they did not care whether she was Muslim or not. They continued ransacking the house; meanwhile Som Anand had come back from his friend's house; he was accompanied by his cousin Pran (Dr G.P. Talwar, the famous Indian immunologist). They immediately decided to send Pran to call Gurkha soldiers from Model Town Club. The Gurkhas came immediately and chased the mob away.

Upon reaching home in the evening, Anand got to know about the day's happenings and how Maulvi Ahmad and his wife had saved his family from the murderous Pathans. He thanked them wholeheartedly. As a result of this incident, he reluctantly decided to leave Lahore and move to Delhi. He decided to hand over all the bank ownership documents to his friend Hafeez Jalandhari (a famous poet who wrote Pakistan's national anthem and was also regarded as the Rabindranath Tagore of Pakistan) for safe custody. He then boarded a flight to Delhi with his entire family, leaving behind Lahore and Model Town forever.

'Chaley Gaye Heerey, Aa Gaye Kheere'

Although Fakirchand Anand physically relocated to Delhi, his heart still resided in Lahore. His son Som Anand has written in his memoir *Lahore 1947** that his father was deeply entangled in bank disputes. Even after Partition, Hafeez Jalandhari frequently called his father to resolve all the disputes of the bank. Anand, at first, visited Lahore and stayed there for only a few weeks to help in the resolution. But later, he decided to stay there till the matter was completely resolved. He stayed in the same old house in Model Town, but now the title of ownership of the house was held by his dear friend, Aziz Baksh. Fakirchand Anand had given away that house to Aziz, and he stayed there for a few months till the legal matter concerning the documents was resolved. Som Anand, who would come to meet his father, also stayed there during his visits. According to Som, the place had completely changed after Partition. Neither was Lahore the same nor was its vibe. It had completely lost its identity. Old residents of Model Town were not at all happy with the occupancy of the old houses by the new migrants.

Model Town had lost its 'upper-class aura'. Old residents of the locality missed the dignified and highly educated residents who lived there earlier.

Som said that when he had gone to Model Town to stay for some time a few years after Partition, he had suddenly heard a

---

*   A. Salim and M. Amruddin, Lahore 1947, An Unforgettable August, 2nd ed., Tara Press, 2006, pp. 133

familiar voice that sounded like that of the vegetable vendor who used to ply his trade there during the pre-Partition days. Som rushed out of the house in excitement to see who it was and, to his surprise, it was indeed the same old vendor pulling his old cart of vegetables and shouting '*Chaley gaye heerey, aa gaye kheere*' which meant that the diamonds had been replaced by cucumbers! Som couldn't control his laughter at that.

Som has also mentioned in his memoir that the one person who was very upset with the Hindu and Sikh residents leaving Model Town was Maulvi Ahmad's wife. Though she had no personal enmity with her new neighbours, she didn't get along with any of them. She felt as if the city of Lahore had lost its true identity and culture following the emigration of the Hindus and Sikhs. She said that when she, along with other women, would travel in a bus, fellow Hindu and Sikh passengers vacated their seats for them to sit as they had great manners. But she found the new residents to be nowhere near them when it came to showing such courtesy towards women; she always cursed how Partition had changed their way of life.

4

The Lost Blazer of Dr G.P. Talwar

I am now going to share with you the story of Padma Bhushan awardee Dr G.P. Talwar, aka Pran Talwar, who should be hailed for eradicating the disease of leprosy. He was the one who developed the Mycobacterium w (*Mw*) vaccine and established the National Institute of Immunology under the leadership and guidance of Indira Gandhi, the then prime minister of India. Talwar also made a major contribution to society by establishing and successfully operating the most prestigious medical science institute in India, the All India Institute of Medical Sciences (AIIMS) in 1956. Even today, at the age of ninety-four, he does research work in the field of vaccines and immunocontraception at the Talwar Research Foundation based in Neb Valley, Delhi.

If you remember the Urdu journalist Som Anand, the son of Fakirchand Anand, from the previous chapter, then you will recall that I had mentioned one of his relatives, Pran, in the story. Back in 1947, in the Model Town locality of Lahore, when Som Anand's house was attacked and vandalized by the Pathans, Pran was present there. It was Pran who had rushed to the Model Town Club to seek the help of the Gorkha soldiers, as a result of which, many lives were saved. At the time, Pran was just twenty-one years old.

When I enquired about Pran from the former doctors at AIIMS, they said that even at the age of ninety-four, he is physically very active and works like a young person. He is very fond of wearing attractive and fashionable clothes and does not let his lifestyle reflect his age. I once got in touch with him over the phone, expecting to hear an aged person's voice from the other end. But I was pleasantly amazed by his youthful tone when I spoke to him. He said that despite the country being under a lockdown due to COVID-19, he still meets people, the reason being his professional involvement in the development of vaccines for such viruses. And that this virus was similar to other viruses in the most basic and characteristic way. He said that he regularly visited India International Centre near Lodhi Garden. 'If you want, I can meet you over there, but if it is still closed, you can come to my place', he said. I went to his farmhouse in Neb Valley. He has two bungalows there. In one of the bungalows, Dr Talwar lives with his wife, and in the other, he runs his Talwar Research Foundation. His son and one of his daughters live overseas and his other daughter lives in Delhi. When I reached his place, he was prepped and ready to receive me. He offered me some scotch from his tasteful collection and started narrating his story.

According to Dr Talwar, aka Pran, his father, Dinanath, used to reside at Firozpur Road in Lahore, but later, he built a bungalow in Model Town and shifted there. He married three times and Pran was born to his second wife. His father ran a medicine manufacturing company named Eastern Pharmaceutical Company. Maybe that was the reason Pran, after completing his BSc (Hons) in chemistry, decided to pursue MSc (Technology) from a government college in Punjab University, Lahore. He was a very good athlete and served as captain of his college team. He had been awarded many trophies and certificates in the field of sports.

Partition and Parting from Family

While he was pursuing his post-graduate degree, Pran had gone
to Kangra, Himachal Pradesh, from Lahore for a two-month
internship/training at a factory. When he was in Kangra, he got
to know about the partition of the country and that people were
being massacred in large numbers. His family members were in
Lahore, with whom he was unable to establish any contact over the
phone; consequently, Pran decided to go back to Lahore himself.
He somehow reached Hoshiarpur by hanging onto the roof of a
truck since roads on one side were closed and cars were not plying.
As for the trains, it was very dangerous to travel in them since
they were being stopped on their way and people on board were
being brutally killed by the rioters on both the sides of the newly
announced border.

When Pran reached Hoshiarpur, people told him he was
playing with fire, going to Lahore in these turbulent times. 'You are
lucky that you decided to come here [Hoshiarpur], now mentally
prepare yourself to live here and let go of the thoughts to know
the whereabouts of your family.' In great despair, Pran took shelter
at a friend's house and was well taken care of there. After a few
days, Pran left his friend's place and managed to somehow reach
Jalandhar, travelling by foot, a bullock cart and a truck, and spent
many days at his relative's place. Thereafter, he went to Amritsar,
where he was told that he could not go to Lahore at any cost since
everything had been shut and the city was witnessing intense
violence. But Pran Talwar turned a deaf ear to all the warnings and
was very firm with his decision. He barged into the office of the
deputy commissioner and started pleading with him to help him
reach Lahore to meet his family. The officer, out of compassion,
agreed to help him and said that he would send him to Lahore in
an army lorry, but in exchange, he would have to volunteer for a
task. 'Once you reach there, you will have to identify all the Sikh
and Hindu families who are stuck in Lahore due to the riots and

send them back to Amritsar safely in our trucks', he said. Pran agreed. Finally, he made it to Model Town in Lahore.

When Pran entered his house in Lahore, he was shocked. The house had been completely vandalized and looted—nothing was left behind; he was surprised to see that the rioters had even taken away all his medals and trophies. Not even a single member of the family was present in the house and the eerie silence was painful for Pran to bear. Pran's biological mother had already passed away when he was just six days old; he had been raised by his stepmother. Now, following the riots, he was really worried about his father and praying for his safety. When he asked around about his family, he came to know that his family had gone to Dayal Bagh in Agra. One of Pran's paternal aunts resided in a Radha Swami hermitage in Agra; the whole family was part of that community. Pran heaved a sigh of relief, hoping his family had reached there safely. Nothing was left in his old house and there was a danger of rioters attacking the place again to kill him. With these things in mind, he rushed to one of his relative's place. Lala Fakirchand Anand, who was the owner of a private bank in Lahore, was wealthy and well respected. Fakirchand took Pran under his wing and ensured his safety and comfort, but after two days, Fakirchand became worried and felt Pran was not safe at his place. Moreover, one of his Muslim friends who had come from Kapurthala was living with his family at Fakirchand's house. Therefore, he was sure about his own safety. Fakirchand requested one of his friends, Hafeez Jalandhari, who was residing nearby, to provide shelter to Pran. Hafeez was hospitable and treated Pran like his own son. He made Pran stay in the section of the house meant only for female members of the family (known as Janaankhana). Men were not allowed to enter this section. Similarly, the Mardaankhana of the house was meant for the male members of the family. Pran started living in the Janaankhana, where Hafeez's wife looked after him with affection.

Now Pran Talwar recalled the task assigned by the deputy commissioner who helped him reach Lahore. For this purpose, he grew his beard and arranged for a Muslim sherwani and cap. Pran would step out of the house as a Muslim in the morning and prepare a list of all the Hindu and Sikh families trapped in Lahore due to the riots, and by evening, he would help in sending them to Amritsar in an army truck or lorry. The interesting part was that Pran did this work while staying with Hafeez Jalandhari, who was not only proud of him for doing so but also encouraged him.

Pran recalls an incident when he once visited a small Hindu family of a father and son in Model Town, Lahore. He said to them, 'I have written your name in the list. You can leave for Amritsar in the army truck.' But the father and son refused to go anywhere. The father told Pran that he had built his house with the savings of his entire life and that he could not let it go. He felt the riots would stop in a few days. Pran tried to convince them of the dire consequences if they did not leave, but they refused to listen to him. The truck came to their house on the second day as well, but they did not leave. On the third day, when Pran went to their house to convince them once again, he was shocked to find the father and son lying dead, their bodies covered in blood. He has not forgotten that scene even today, he says, and felt very sorry for them. Had they decided to leave their house, they could have survived; but the father's emotional attachment to the house did not let them leave Lahore safely.

Pran had become closed to Fakirchand Anand's son, Som Anand, who was the same age as him. One day, they were at a friend's place. His name was Ata Mohammad. It was then that Fakirchand Anand's house was attacked. The rioters ignored the fact that there was another Muslim family living in that house. They looted Fakirchand's house. This is when Pran rushed to Model Town Club to call on the Gorkha soldiers for help and saved the lives of Fakirchand's family members. Pran, now Dr G.P. Talwar, told me that he saved hundreds of Hindus and Sikhs and sent them to Amritsar in army trucks.

From Lahore to Amritsar to Paris to Germany

After carrying out the task of saving the Hindu and Sikh families from rioters in Lahore, Pran eventually decided to leave that city once and for all. He reached Amritsar in an army truck. From there, he went to Dayal Bagh in Agra, where he found his father, stepmother and stepbrother living in a very small place. Pran's stepmother's attitude towards him was not welcoming at all. Pran realized that he would not be able to move ahead in life in this manner, so he decided to shift to Delhi and went to his maternal aunt's (maasi) place in Rajpur Road. Her husband was the owner of Traders Bank. Thereafter, he was taken care of by her like her own son. The good doctor still feels immensely grateful to her.

When Pran had left Lahore in the middle of his MSc (Technology) course for an internship in Kangra, his final examinations were yet to be conducted. After coming to India, he had inquired about his studies, which he wished to complete. Pran got to know that a part of Punjab University had become a part of India after Partition. The regional offices of the university were located in Solan, Himachal Pradesh, and Delhi. He got in touch with the officials, appeared for the examinations and was finally awarded the master's degree. However, struggle was still a part of his life. He worked with Sehgal and Company for Rs 200 a month in Connaught Place (CP), Delhi. The company used to import and sell paper.

Pran used to commute from Rajpur Road to CP on a bicycle and in the evenings, he would have a cup of tea with his very dear friend Madanjeet Singh at Kwality restaurant in CP. One day, they got to know through the newspapers that some foreign scholarships had been advertised. Both Pran and Madanjeet filled the forms and soon found themselves preparing for a new chapter of their lives as Madanjeet got a scholarship to study in Italy and Pran got one to go to France.

Pran reached France's Marseille Fos Port via ship and from there he went to Paris. He got to work at one of the most prestigious institutes of France, the Pasteur Institute, where the process of making champagne was researched and improved for the producers in a region in France known as Champagne.

Pran studied chemical engineering at the same institute and planned to set up a distillery in India. Whenever he went on a visit to the champagne factories, he was supposed to taste the champagne and comment on the quality. He never liked the taste of the drink. So the officials of the institute transferred him to the microbiology department, where he was awarded the degree of Doctor of Science and an extended fellowship. He worked in an important position in Paris and then went to Germany to conduct some research work with a Nobel prize winner in the year 1953. Syed Haider Raza, the famous painter, used to reside in the same hostel in Paris as Pran. While leaving Paris, he had gifted one of his paintings to Pran, which is still present in his bungalow at Neb Valley. Most of the people who are in the business of buying and selling paintings still contact him to buy that painting at any price, but Pran is not willing to sell that token of memory.

Indira Gandhi and AIIMS

When he was residing in Germany, Pran saw an advertisement in the newspapers that the government of India, under the leadership of Pandit Nehru, wanted to set up a medical institution recognized and funded by the central government. This institution went on to become the renowned All India Institute of Medical Sciences. The institute then needed specialists, for which an ad appeared in the newspapers. Pran Talwar also filled an application for the same and the committee, with A. Lakshmanaswami Mudaliar (famous educationist and physician) as its chairman, selected him. According to the former doctors of AIIMS, Dr Har Gobind Khorana (Indian-American biochemist) had also appeared for an interview, but instead of him, the committee selected Dr Talwar. Later, Khorana was awarded a Nobel prize for physiology in America.

Pran's maternal aunt (maasi) was pressuring him to return home, and in the year 1956, when he landed on Indian soil, he was supposed to join AIIMS for work on 9 August. He was told that AIIMS was situated near the Safdarjung airport, ahead of a railway line constructed near it, but when he reached, he could not see the building of the institute. Suddenly, his attention was drawn towards a neem tree with a small board tied around it. 'AIIMS' was written on this board. He saw that two apartments in a building had been turned into offices. He was shocked as he had attended two of the most prestigious institutes in Paris and Germany, but returned to see the world-famous Indian institute under construction. When he entered the building, he saw that his secretary, K.C.K.E. Raja, was sitting at a big desk that had been donated by Rajkumari Amrit Kaur (Indian activist and politician, and the first health minister of India). Pran was made the head of the biochemistry department, the classes for which commenced in the hostel of the nurses. Pran was also awarded the Nehru fellowship, whose chairperson was Indira Gandhi. Even though she was the prime minister of the country, she used to meet the Nehru fellows at least once a year at her office in Teen Murti Bhawan, Delhi, and spent almost half the day with them.

One day, in the year 1983, Indira Gandhi asked Dr Talwar about vaccines in a meeting. He replied that many vaccines which could save the lives of people of almost all age groups could be developed. After ten days, Indira Gandhi asked for the National Institute of Immunology to be set up. Dr Talwar was handed the task of formally establishing it within two years and running it subsequently. Unfortunately, by the time the institute became functional, Indira Gandhi had been assassinated, and later, Rajiv Gandhi inaugurated the institute. It was here that Dr Talwar developed the Mycobacterium w (*Mw*) vaccine for treating leprosy. Apart from treating leprosy, this vaccine is also being used by pharmaceutical companies for curing many other life-threatening diseases today.

Looking Back

I asked Dr Talwar whether he ever visited Lahore again. He replied that he had in the year 1992 for a conference. There was a grand welcome ceremony. He requested for a visit to his old government college and the officials arranged for the same. He said that when he reached there, all his old memories came rushing back. It was vacation time when he had visited but the dean was present at the premises. He warmly welcomed and greeted him. Pran narrated the entire story to the dean about how the rioters had looted all of his medals, certificates and even the blazer that had the monogram of the college printed on it from his house in Lahore. I asked him if he visited his house in Model Town, and he replied that he did not feel like going there. 'When everything is gone from there, what is the need for me to visit that place now?' I agreed with what he said. He then said that there was one thing that happened that he really liked. A few days after he returned to Delhi he received a parcel from his college in Lahore. It was a blazer with the monogram of the college. Not only that, but they had also reissued all the certificates from the records of the university that he had lost in the riots.

5

A Journey to Lahore

Syyed Imtiaz Humayun

My interactions with people in Pakistan apprised me of numerous stories of Partition. One story that has all the elements of a potential Bollywood script pertains to Syyed Imtiaz Humayun, who narrated it to me during one of my visits to Lahore. He was about ninety then. Listening to his story, I could still feel what he went through because even at his age, it was ingrained so deeply in his memory.

Syyed Imtiaz Humayun was sixteen years old when he finished high school in Peshawar and secured the first division. His father, who was serving as deputy accountant general, made up his mind to send him to Bombay for further studies. He had a friendly relation with J.W. Kwain, the principal of St Xavier's College, Bombay. Admitted as a special case, Imtiaz completed his graduation there. For accommodation he rented a room near Dhobi Talao, Bombay. During this time, in 1945, Imtiaz got married to the daughter of Syyed Nadir Hussain, who lived in Delhi. Nadir Hussain had a flourishing timber business there. He also loved to play cricket and was among the top cricket players in Delhi. Imtiaz Humayun's

43

family on the other hand was based in Jalandhar, where they were among the well-known and wealthy landlords. Hundreds of acres of lands belonged to them, and his grandfather—Qazi Syyed Mehboob Aalam—was also a well-known and well-regarded personality of Jalandhar. He was often addressed as the archduke of Jalandhar. He had a huge bungalow near the railway station there. He owned many *ber* (jujube fruit) gardens that were contracted to cultivators every year. Qazi was the father of six girls and three boys. In the days when people considered only their sons eligible to become heirs to their wealth, he had left one bungalow in each of his daughters' names. He was well-respected by the Hindus and followed a strict principle—if there was any dispute between Hindus and Muslims on any issue, Qazi and the chief priest of the temple would take the final decision on the matter together. Qazi used to live in Mohalla Kazia, which was quite a peaceful area, and people never fought among each other there.

He was a firm supporter of the Congress and was direly against Muhammad Ali Jinnah. Every weekend he used to visit the Company Gardens Club to play bridge. During one such visit, he came across Jinnah and scolded him, saying, 'You are a public figure, a leader of the *avaam* (common people), don't you feel ashamed of yourself that you roam around in clubs? Look at Gandhi, he is walking hand in hand with the poor and common people and is trying his best to understand their problems and is working for their upliftment.' Jinnah was furious at this and said he did not want to be like Gandhi. He said he was one of those people who cannot bear a single spot of dirt on their collar, which is to say that he could not bear any blot on his conscience. He did not want to conduct his politics in the manner of Gandhi. Listening to his words, Qazi's anger flared up and he told me he gave another earful to Jinnah and headed out of the club.

I do not know whether Qazi's impression of Jinnah was right or wrong, but I can definitely relate to M.J. Akbar's impression (famous journalist and author) related in his recent book *Gandhi's Hinduism: The Struggle against Jinnah's Islam*. There he has narrated an incident that goes like this:

Jinnah, in spite of being a famous figure in the struggle for independence, never went to prison. Once when someone put forth this question to him, 'Why have you never been imprisoned and sent to jail?', he gave a very blunt reply, 'Am I some thief or goon that I would go to jail?' Jinnah had always been on good terms with the British, and they never gave orders to arrest him or to send him to jail. Not only that, Jinnah took a step back from the great struggle for freedom and settled in London, where he started practising law. Earlier, he had been against the ideologies of the Muslim League and always preached about unity between Hindus and Muslims; but later when he realized that he could make a separate country with the help of the Muslim League and also rule it, he returned to India to join the Muslim League and became its leader. According to M.J. Akbar, in one of the conferences organized by the Muslim League, Jinnah spoke ill of Gandhi and vilified him as a leader of only the Hindus and an enemy of the Muslims; this is where he put forward his demand for a separate country. Gandhi sent him a letter from jail which read, 'I am ready to meet you in jail to discuss and seek clarification on this allegation. Please come and meet me.' At the time, the British thought that if Gandhi and Jinnah were to meet, they might unite again, and the Partition would be deferred. That is the reason Churchill, who was in Washington then, asked the Indian viceroy to make sure that this meeting never took place. As a consequence, Gandhi's letter was not dispatched from jail and never reached Jinnah. Gandhi had accepted the challenge through that letter and, according to Akbar, had Jinnah received the letter, Jinnah would have, at least once, seen the insides of a jail in his lifetime even if it was just to meet Gandhi. But as destiny would have it, it did not happen.

The Case of the Peshawari Slippers

Qazi had been reluctant to go to Pakistan even during Partition and wanted to stay in Jalandhar in India, but when the riots started raging, he had to leave for Pakistan under the mounting pressure of his relatives and family members. He certainly did not get close to the quantum of land and properties that he owned in Jalandhar in his new country, but he got a bungalow to live in and a few plots of land. In Rawalpindi, he was allotted a soda factory by the government, but due to some impending legal issues, he was never given possession of it. However, the then prime minister (*Wazir-e-Aazam*) Liaquat Ali Khan was in favour of allotting this factory to him. Yakub Ali Khan, who later became the chief justice of Pakistan, was Qazi's lawyer. Qazi was given the Galaxy Cinema Hall in Lahore along with 30 *kanal* (18,000 square yards) of land. He also got a bungalow on Badat Road in Lahore, but later he made his residence in a bungalow near Galaxy Cinema on Ferozpur Road. When Qazi passed away, he had 101 grandsons, granddaughters, great-grandsons and great-granddaughters cumulatively.

Qazi's spirit of secularism can be highlighted from an incident involving a close friend of his, Lala, who once visited Jalandhar to get his sword sharpened. The boy who was supposed to do the task asked him, 'Lalaji, why are you getting your sword sharpened?' In plain humour, Lala replied, 'I want to kill Quaid-e-Azam.' Later, when Lala went to collect his sword, the boy murdered Lala with the same sword. When Qazi got to know about this incident, he took every possible step to make sure the boy was arrested. He was later sentenced to life imprisonment for the murder. It was Qazi's lawyer, Yakub Ali Khan, who was the prosecuting attorney at the court during his trial.

I will now circle back to tell you further about Imtiaz Humayun, who was the grandchild of Qazi. While he was pursuing his studies in Bombay, an interesting episode occurred. He met Prithviraj Kapoor, one of the pioneers of Indian theatre and the Hindi film industry. Kapoor invited him for a screen test at Kala Mandir in Bombay and offered him the role of a villain in a film. When Imtiaz expressed his disagreement, Kapoor explained to him that while he looked like a handsome hero in real life, on camera his face better suited that of a villain. Imtiaz turned down the offer and continued to focus on his studies. During this time, political discussions on Partition reached an advanced stage. Reports of communal riots started surfacing from many cities across the country. One day, Imtiaz received a letter from his father in which he was informed of their overnight departure from Jalandhar to Pakistan; the letter also stated that they would most likely go to Lahore and that Imtiaz's wife was going with them. Communication via phones was not available in those days. This sudden event crushed young Imtiaz under a mountain of stress and left him clueless about what he should do next. He was completely unaware of the whereabouts of his family members—had they reached Lahore safely or had they been massacred on the way? There were no means of communication—neither Imtiaz's family nor Imtiaz could send or receive letters. Horrifying riots were taking place. Everything was shut. Imtiaz spent the evenings at Marine Drive gloomily sitting by the seashore for hours and went home to spend sleepless nights. He was in despair and had completely lost hope of meeting his wife and family members ever again.

One of his relatives, Fayaz Hussain, resided near Marine Drive. Imtiaz visited their house to seek his advice as to what his next step should be. His relative suggested that he forget about his family and move on. He suggested that if Imtiaz wanted to stay alive, he should settle in India permanently, because he would not survive if he tried to go back to Jalandhar to look for his family. Imtiaz came back with despair in his eyes and a pale face. The memories of his loved ones were flashing before him; he could not let their memories simply fade away. Finally, the young boy decided not to bother about his life and went on a quest to reunite with his family, which is what mattered to him the most. He boarded a train for Delhi and the very next day; when the train stopped at Jhansi station, the rioters entered the train and started searching it thoroughly for any Muslim passenger. Though as a young Muslim boy, he was scared and anxious, he tried his best to be calm and sit quietly. A person sitting right in front of him named Gopal Das, who was a Hindu businessman, asked Imtiaz, 'Beta, who are you? Hindu or Muslim?' He replied anxiously, 'I am a Hindu.' To which Gopal Das said, 'Don't be afraid. I know you are a Muslim since you are wearing Peshawari slippers. You should quickly go to the toilet and throw these slippers out and wear mine instead.' After some time, the rioters entered their coach. They approached Gopal Das and asked his name and he identified himself. Thereafter, they asked about Imtiaz, and Gopal Das introduced Imtiaz as his son, Shyam. They stared at Imtiaz briefly but then moved on. The train left from Jhansi and reached Delhi station. Gopal Das deboarded the train bare-footed and moved on to his destination. He gave Imtiaz—whom he had turned into his son, Shyam—his blessings, and invited him to his home. But Imtiaz was eager to meet his own family. He apologized and touched Gopal Das's feet. Gopal Das then gave him some money to take care of his expenses for the journey ahead.

Saharanpur

At the Delhi station, Imtiaz was sitting numb while he waited for a train to Jalandhar. The officers at the railway station informed him that the trains to Punjab had been cancelled due to the riots. People were stopping the trains on their way and brutally massacring the passengers. Imtiaz was not able to figure out what to do next. Suddenly, he remembered that his maternal uncle lived in Saharanpur in Uttar Pradesh. He enquired with the railway officials about trains going there. They confirmed that trains to Saharanpur were going as there were no riots on that route. He immediately boarded a train to go to his maternal uncle Maksood

Aalam's place. His uncle took Imtiaz in. He too was completely unaware of the whereabouts of his sister and brother-in-law in Jalandhar. According to Imtiaz, where on the one hand northern India was witnessing riots between the Hindus and the Muslims, Saharanpur was one place where there was complete harmony. Hindus and Muslims were living together peacefully and people from both communities stood by each other's side and protected each other. Looking at the peaceful atmosphere of Saharanpur, the resident Muslims refused to accept Pakistan at any cost as their country and had decided that no Muslim from Saharanpur would go to Pakistan.

A well-known wrestler from Saharanpur named Bundu, who was very tall and had a strong build, was asked by one of the leaders of the Muslim League, Shah Nazar, who had very close ties with him, to come along to Pakistan; but Bundu refused. Shah Nazar had promised to reward him with a high post in the government of Pakistan as bait. However, Bundu turned down the offer and chose to live in Saharanpur, in poverty, till he was 120 years old and finally passed away in 2007.

This was the uniqueness of Saharanpur. At one point in time, Imtiaz had also tried to convince his maternal uncle to go to Pakistan since he knew he was rich and politically influential. Imtiaz had a hidden agenda behind this; he thought he could safely reach Pakistan in their car, but his maternal uncle was not ready to go at any cost. Imtiaz could not comprehend what to do. He was now left with no option but to travel alone. Imtiaz missed his family every moment he spent in Saharanpur. Almost a month had passed and Imtiaz had begun to feel as if his maternal uncle was least bothered about his family. Everyone was busy with their own lives. Imtiaz came to know that the army depot in Saharanpur was sending Muslim army men, those who wished to go, to Pakistan in their army trucks. He went to the army depot, but the British officers there refused to send him to Pakistan as only army people were allowed in the truck and not civilians. Imtiaz started

sobbing as he lost another ray of hope of meeting his family. The
dangerous idea of attempting to go by train crossed his mind.
When he reached the railway station, the moment the train from
Delhi to Punjab arrived, he heard an announcement, 'All Muslim
passengers are advised to deboard the train at Saharanpur itself
since the situation in Punjab has deteriorated and Muslims are
not safe there anymore.' Listening to this, Imtiaz again went back
to his maternal uncle's house and was depressed all night long.
The very next day, he went to the army depot where he had met a
Hindu second-lieutenant officer. He begged him to allow him to
go and narrated his entire story—how his parents and wife had got
separated from him, and so on. He showed him all the letters that
his family had sent. Listening to Imtiaz, the officer was overcome
with compassion. He agreed to send Imtiaz in the truck disguised
as an army man. 'But the problem is that if the fellow officers in
the truck ask you anything, you might get caught. Therefore, I
will train you for two days on how to answer their questions and in
the language of the army.' And so he did. He taught Imtiaz in the
next two days—his post, his 'core', his exact work in the army, his
commanding officer and other such minute details. On the third
day, Imtiaz was dressed in army uniform and put in the truck. He
was told to sit quietly in the truck and not talk to anyone. When the
truck reached Ambala, he threw away his suitcase so that he was
not caught and recognized by anyone. According to Imtiaz, people
were being slaughtered at Phagwara and Jalandhar. The Sikhs
were stopping the trucks on their way and thoroughly searching
for Muslims. Somehow, their truck made its way through these
cities, but in Amritsar, the Sikhs had deployed barricades and their
truck was stopped. The army men were frightened, but the senior
officer sitting in the front seat showed them the permission letter
from Delhi and warned the rioters that if they were made to wait
for more than five minutes, he would give orders to fire at them.
Afraid, the group of Sikh rioters backed off and made way for
the army truck.

On their way to Jalandhar, there was intense violence in the Phillaur district. There were many Sikh-dominated villages nearby, and the villagers were on a killing spree. According to Imtiaz, it was 2 a.m. when his truck reached close to the old airport in Walton Camp in Lahore. Every passenger of the truck disembarked at that point. Imtiaz heaved a sigh of relief at being alive still. He was finally in Pakistan. He was very happy. He then slid away quietly and started eating some chickpeas that he was carrying in his pocket. He went on his way to his final destination, happy and whistling. Imtiaz visited three of his relatives in Lahore and asked them about his family members, but none of them knew anything about his family. Then he decided to visit one of his distant relatives as well, who was residing at 4, Mojang Road. At 5 a.m., when he called out his father's name from outside the relative's house, Imtiaz's wife came rushing out of the house and embraced him. And then, all other members of the family gathered and started crying with happiness. They had assumed Imtiaz had been killed in the ongoing violence.

According to Imtiaz, it was a posh locality where many bungalows built by the Hindus and the Sikhs were abandoned, along with their belongings. All those who came from India had captured those bungalows. His family had captured one that belonged to Sardar Charan Singh. Even after Partition, Charan Singh used to visit that place at least three to four times a year to see the house to which he was still emotionally attached. Whenever he visited, Imtiaz's family would take good care of him and Singh was very happy with the way the house was being maintained. Later on, Imtiaz's family sold the house to Mahmud Ali Kasuri, whose son Khurshid Mahmud Kasuri went on to become the foreign minister of Pakistan.

Imtiaz told me that there were countless properties abandoned by people in Lahore. One after the other, the houses were being captured by people who came from India, and moreover, the rehabilitation officers at that time were drafting property documents

in exchange for hefty bribes. During those days, Model Town was
the best among all the new localities. People were scrambling to
capture the houses there, but by that time the government had
come to know about this and they instantly seized all the houses,
and later sold all of them through auction. Old Anarkali, New
Anarkali, Bhaati Gate, Ichra, Sant Nagar, Shah Alami, Krishan
Nagar, Gwalmandi, Harbanshpura and Muglapara were the places
where many Hindus and Sikhs had abandoned their houses.

Now, you might ask me how I met Imtiaz Humayun. When
I visited Lahore in 2004 for the Indo-Pak cricket match series, I
met a young man named Yawar Salman, who belonged to a very
well-reputed, educated and affluent family at a party organized
by a famous socialite of Lahore, Sabina Sehgal. Imtiaz Humayun
was the maternal grandfather (nana) of Yawar Salman. Yawar
arranged my meeting with him at his place in 2008. He had aged,
but Imtiaz narrated his entire story to me in great detail. He had
a very strong memory. He told me that after coming to Lahore
from Bombay, he worked with Eastern Federal Union Insurance
Company from where he would get Rs 250 per month. He did not
hesitate to tell me that J.W. Kwine, the principal of his college, St.
Xavier's, had issued him a fake certificate that said Imtiaz studied
in their college and that he was working for Eastern Federal
Union Insurance Company in Bombay. On the basis of this, the
insurance company in Lahore offered him a job. But in reality he
had only been studying in Bombay and never worked anywhere.

Later, he was transferred to Dhaka in East Pakistan. Imitiaz
said that the people of West Pakistan, especially people from
Punjab, used to hate East Pakistan and could never tolerate the
people of Bengal. They used to treat them as outsiders. He had to
spend a long time in Dhaka, but he never liked working with the
people of erstwhile East Bengal; so he resigned and returned to
Lahore. Imtiaz's son got married to the daughter of S.A. Rehman,
who had once served as chief justice of Pakistan. Salman Siddique,
Yawar's father, who was a bureaucrat and served as finance

secretary of Pakistan, also later served as the chief secretary of the Punjab State in Pakistan.

Though his journey from Jalandhar to Lahore was full of difficulties and challenges, it made the remaining part of his life fulfilling. He passed away in 2010, and the respect he had for India never faded from his heart.

Shekhupura

Yawar Salman, the grandson of Imtiaz, has also become a successful businessman in Lahore. Apart from his business in the telecom sector, he supplies goods to the Afghan military and has purchased a farmhouse near the Wagah border.

Yawar's elder brother Ali Salman is currently a minister in Punjab from Imran Khan's party. Yawar and Ali took me to his village called Manawala once, and on the way, there was a place called Shekhupura.

Shekhupura is named after the son of Akbar, Jahangir, aka Shekhu. Akbar used to scold his son Jahangir for being a womanizer and an alcoholic. Jahangir was angry about this and decided not live in the fort of Lahore. Around 40 kilometres away from Lahore, he built a small palace with a garden and a lake. He lived there and used to go hunting from there. Jahangir had built this luxurious palace just to stay away from his father. Although he hunted down animals in the jungle, he had a deer whom he loved very much and nurtured him as a pet. One day, the deer passed away, leaving Shekhu in mourning; he did not eat anything for two days. Near the lake, Jahangir had built a mausoleum for his deer, which people visited from different places.

Jahangir and Anarkali's love story is another well-known story; some narratives suggest that Akbar had buried Anarkali in a wall to keep her away from Jahangir. Others say that he had built a fake wall behind Anarkali and helped her escape through it. However, nobody knows to what extent these stories are true, but

Anarkali's grave is inside a building made up of very old stones in the secretariat building of Punjab government. Although civilians are not allowed to enter the building, Yawar was able to show me that historic structure, Anarkali's tomb, since his father Salman Siddique's office was inside that building.

Yawar also showed me Lahore Fort where the Darbaar-e-aam is still as it was; Akbar used to sit on a raised platform and the common people would gather in a huge open hall. When Atal Bihari Vajpayee visited Lahore as the prime minister, Nawaz Sharif had hosted a gala dinner in his honour at the Lahore Fort. In his speech, Vajpayee mentioned the fort as historic, the place where Akbar lived as the ruler for about sixteen years and where all the major events of his life occurred.

The fort has the tombstone of Luv–Kush (sons of Lord Rama) and according to the Lahore municipality documents, the city of Lahore is named after Luv. The Lahore fort housed the tomb of Raja Ranjit Singh and Guru Arjun Dev, the great Sikh guru. Also, this fort used to be at the base of River Ravi, but now the river has changed its course and does not flow through here.

Yawar's paternal grandfather, Raja Mohammad Siddique, was a landlord in Hoshiarpur, Punjab (India) who moved to Manawala village of Shekhupura district after Partition, where he got vast tracts of land. They were originally Rajputs before converting to Islam, and that is why he used 'Raja' as a title before his Muslim name.

Yawar also took me to Gujranwala, which is around 80 kilometres from Lahore, for sightseeing. This city is known for its wrestlers. I could see wrestling arenas all over the city. Maharana Ranjit Singh used to live here and later his birthplace was converted into a gurudwara. I told Yawar that I would like to see Maharana Ranjit Singh's birthplace. Upon reaching there, I was shocked to see that the gurudwara had been turned into a police station. The place where the chief priest of the gurudwara used to sit was now the cabin of the station house officer, and the room where Ranjit Singh was born had been converted into a lock-up for criminals. The chief police officer took us for a tour of the police station. Looking at this, I felt very bad. When I returned to Lahore, I told everything to the chief secretary, Salman Siddique, father of Yawar. He advised me to speak to Chief Minister Parvez Ilahi. Incidentally, at that time, the then tourism minister of India, Ambika Soni, was in Lahore. She was staying at the Governor House. Along with her, I approached the chief minister, who had always wanted Pakistan to maintain cordial relations with India. He immediately passed the order to restore the place to a gurudwara.

Yawar had also taken me to Kuku Café, which was located in the Heeramandi area in front of the fort. Speaking of which, this area is famous for being home to hundreds of sex workers. Many brothels are operated there, but the area is divided into two parts. One part is designated as brothels, but in the second part there are only establishments which host mujras. Even the most well-read and civilized people of Lahore come here to enjoy the dance; in the areas where the ladies perform mujra, no unsocial or illegal activities take place. People come here to enjoy only the songs and dance perfomances and these ladies do not resort to any kind of activities that are considered illegal. Nowadays, in Pakistan, people organize mujras in the comfort of their homes with their family members. Coming back to Kuku Café, it belongs to the son of one such prostitute from Heeramandi. He has maintained the building as it was and has retained everything in its original form. Idols of Lord Ganesha and Lord Shiva have been kept everywhere and the café serves scrumptious food and coffee.

There is a story about the famous poets Firaq Gorakhpuri and Faiz Ahmad Faiz. They were good friends and quite learned in the English language but were poets of Urdu. After many years of Partition, Firaq Gorakhpuri aka Raghupati Sahay Srivastav went to Lahore from Allahabad to meet his friend. Faiz sahab warmly welcomed him and took him to Heeramandi for watching a mujra so that he could see the classical song and dance form of Pakistani culture. The moment the dance began, Firaq sahab asked for some liquor. But when Faiz stopped him saying liquor is prohibited, Firaq sahab got irritated and stood up. Angrily he said, 'This is a weird outcome of the Partition, the beauty remains here and the wines have crossed the border.'

6

Father of an Indian Prime Minister
Avtar Narain Gujral

The family of Avtar Narain Gujral is amongst those who scaled great heights in life with immense hard work and struggle after moving to India from Pakistan after Partition. Avtar Narain, based in Jhelum city of Pakistan, was an advocate by profession and also played an active part in politics. He had been imprisoned during the freedom struggle for the first time under the leadership of Lala Lajpat Rai and many times thereafter under the leadership of Gandhi and Nehru. He was the father to three sons: namely Inder, Raj and Satish Kumar Gujral. Avtar Narain was doing well as an advocate in the city of Jhelum. Right in front of Gujral's house, there was a two-bedroom house where Achint Ram had come to stay from Lahore. Achint Ram worked actively in Lala Lajpat Rai's organization called 'Servants of the People's Society', for a monthly remuneration of Rs 100. Since Achint Ram did not have running water in his house, he used to go with his son Krishna Kant to fetch water from Avtar Narain's house across the street. Satyawati, Achint Ram's wife, would also frequent his house for water to wash dirty clothes. Gradually, members of both the families became good friends, and later, Achint Ram's son, Krishna Kant, served the nation as vice president of India, under whom I got a chance to work as a member of the Rajya Sabha.

Avtar Narain's father, Dunichandra, was a well-to-do deputy tehsildar in Multan. Unfortunately, Gujral's mother passed away in the plague and, thereafter, he shifted to Jammu with his relatives to complete his schooling and later graduated from D.A.V. College, Lahore.

His relatives did not support his studies beyond high school and were completely against him studying further. He nevertheless completed his higher studies, graduated with BA and LLB degrees and started practising law in Jhelum. As an advocate, he adopted the lifestyle of the British. He dressed like them, socialized in clubs and even played badminton. He owned a huge house and a car. His wife hailed from a nearby village and her name was Nida. She changed her name to Pushpa after marriage. Gujral was a follower of Lala Lajpat Rai and an Arya Samaji. Eventually, when Lajpat Rai chose to follow the path of Gandhi, Avtar Narain also followed him and imbibed the principles of the Swadeshi movement. He burnt all his imported clothes and gave up his British lifestyle. Pushpa was very upset with this and was not ready at all to burn her silk sarees and other clothes. She cried at having to do so but had no choice to go against her husband's decision. However, later she felt proud of doing it.

Avtar Narain was in favour of bringing about reforms in Hindu society to such an extent that on the special occasion of Deepawali, he invited around hundred sweepers to his house and offered them food in the utensils that he used. Pushpa was very angry and sold the utensils because all their relatives were threatening to sever ties with them; but once her anger subsided, she subscribed to her husband's belief and both Avtar Narain and his wife stood firm on their belief of uplifting the poor. The passion to help the needy and the destitute was such that every time they stepped out to buy something, they preferred to purchase it from a shopkeeper who was facing a shortage of customers, irrespective of the quality of goods. Moreover, they decided to send their children to a very ordinary school, perhaps one that could be rated poor in terms of infrastructure and other facilities. This was their way of helping their friend Master Deewan Chandra Jhalla, who used to run the two-room school their children attended.

Every year, Avtar Narain used to visit Pahalgam in Jammu & Kashmir for a family vacation. Once, while in Pahalgam, his son, Satish, was playing under a waterfall. Suddenly, Satish slipped and fell on a rock, injuring his foot badly. When he was being treated, Satish was given the wrong medicine, as a result of which he suffered permanent hearing loss. The tale of misfortunes did not end there. A few years after Satish's accident, Gujral's other son, Raj, drowned in the River Jhelum when he was just eleven. Yet, the grief-sticken Gujral did not lose hope. He admitted Satish to a special school meant for the differently abled in Delhi; but Satish ran away from the school and came back to Jhelum. Gujral then got in touch with the then chief minister of Punjab, Sir Sikandar Hayat Khan, and secured admission for Satish in the famous Mayo School of Arts in Lahore, which is currently known as the National College of Arts. This highly prestigious and world-renowned educational institution was established by John Lockwood Kipling, a famous artist and museum curator and father of the famous writer Rudyard Kipling. Khan himself contacted the then principal of the school, Suminder Nath Gupta, to secure Satish's admission.

However, Gujral's wife Pushpa was completely against sending Satish to an arts school. She believed that her son would become a petty carpenter or a craftsman. But her husband stood by his decision. Satish Gujral went on to become a famous painter, sculptor, muralist and writer in the post-Independence era.

Avtar Narain Gujral was part of the procession led by Lala Lajpat Rai in Lahore against the Simon Commission, where the police cracked down on the protesters by resorting to lathicharge

as a result of which Lala Lajpat Rai died. The incident agitated
Bhagat Singh, Rajguru and Sukhdev. After a few months, they
murdered a British police officer named John P. Saunders.

Avtar Narain had a nephew by the name of Onkar who used
to stay with the Gujral family, and Gujral adored him like his
own son. Gujral was shocked when he learnt that he had been
arrested by the police since his name was in the list of persons who
were suspected of conspiring to kill Saunders, along with Bhagat
Singh. Until the arrest, Gujral was unaware that his nephew was
secretly associated with Bhagat Singh in his movement for India's
freedom, and later, he fought his case as his advocate in court in
Lahore for many years.

Later on, Avtar remained active in politics and developed
strong relations with many Congress leaders and with Jinnah too.
Raja Ghazanfar Ali, a well-known Muslim League leader, hailed
from Jhelum and was very close to Jinnah. Gujral and Ghazanfar
Ali were best friends. Before Partition, the interim government of
India was formed with the Muslim League's quota, through which
Ghazanfar served as health minister of India under Jawaharlal
Nehru. In the elections held before Partition in Jhelum, which
was a division of Rawalpindi, Gujral was elected as a member of
the National Assembly. After Partition, his membership fell under
the jurisdiction of the Pakistan National Assembly. Ghazanfar Ali
spoke to Jinnah to ensure that Avtar Narain Gujral held the post
of a minister in the newly formed government of Pakistan. While
Avtar Narain was waiting for his turn to take the oath, intense
riots broke out. Jawaharlal Nehru called him to Lahore urgently
to meet him. Since massive communal riots were going on, Nehru
and Lady Mountbatten also reached Lahore. They were both very
upset with the riots and the migration of people and asked Gujral
and Ghazanfar Ali to control the situation somehow. The very
next day, both Gujral and Ghazanfar returned to Jhelum.

The scenes all around on the way were so horrifying that they
came to terms with the fact that it was impossible to unite the

people now. Raja Ghazanfar Ali wanted the Hindus and Sikhs to continue living in Pakistan, but when the tribals came from Peshawar and began their violent attacks, they lost all hope. Avtar Narain Gujral made his sons, Inder and Satish, undertake a very risky task. They were asked to send the Hindus and Sikhs from Pakistan to India safely in trucks and bring the Muslims from India to Pakistan. By doing this, Inder and Satish saved hundreds of lives. I spoke to both of them and heard the tales. The scenes they described were beyond imagination. According to them, thousands of dead bodies lay on the roads and the stench was so overpowering that it was almost impossible to pass by without throwing up. Trucks had to be driven very cautiously to steer clear of the riot-struck areas. At many places, rioters would attack these trucks on the way and the security personnel were so few that they did not stand a chance in front of the rioting mobs. According to Satish, the students of the Muslim girls' hostel in Amritsar were first paraded naked at the city's Hall Bazaar, following which they were raped and murdered by the Sikhs. Similar treatment was meted out to Hindu and Sikh girls, who were either kidnapped or brutally killed, in Pakistan by the Muslims. Afghani tribals used to dance in Jhelum with rifles in their hands and attack the refugee camps. Gujral, along with his sons, could have fallen prey to such treatment had Raja Ghazanfar Ali not saved them. These tribal men killed women and pierced their children with the bayonet of their rifles and then danced around the bodies to celebrate the inhuman act. Till March 1948, Gujral had saved many people and brought them safely to the refugee camps of Jalandhar and Lahore with help of his sons Inder and Satish.

According to Satish Gujral, a Sikh man and two of his sons were attacked in Khewra town of Jhelum. The father and one of the sons died. The mother somehow saved the other son, but in the haste and panic, she failed to take along her daughter Jaswant Kaur, who was fifteen years old. The girl hid in the backyard of the house where their family had been staying. This house was captured by Ghulam Ishaq, a well-known person of the town. He found the girl hidden in the backyard after three days and decided to give her shelter in his own house since his own daughters were also of the same age. Ghulam Ishaq treated the girl like his own daughter. Meanwhile, the mother of the girl, Kartari, kept searching for her daughter in the refugee camps. Avtar Narain Gujral applied all his might to find the girl. A Muslim soldier informed him that the girl was with Ghulam Ishaq. He immediately got in touch with Ishaq and requested him to return the girl to her mother, but Ishaq refused to do so. He was so adamant that even under the pressure of rioting Muslim mobs to release the Sikh girl, he refused and lied to them that he had married the girl.

Avtar Narain tried his best to convince him but could not succeed. Finally, he sent his security officer, Anwar Khan, to speak to Ghulam Ishaq to allow the girl to meet her mother once. Ghulam, in the meanwhile, fell in love with the girl and started treating her as his wife. Before sending her to meet her mother, Ghulam had physical relations with the girl. After a lot of effort, he agreed to send her to the Jhelum camp to be with her mother. Ghulam used to visit the camp to meet Jaswant every evening till the time she was there. The girl was very attached to her mother and decided to spend the rest of her life with her even though Ghulam Ishaq kept her very well and took care of her. Looking at the entire matter, Gujral decided to send the mother and her children, Jaswant Kaur and Bhagwan Singh, to the Amritsar camp. When Ghulam got to know about this incident, he was very upset. Gujral feared that Ghulam would take revenge, but instead, he started crying and told Gujral that he could not bear the pain of this separation. But now the girl was in India. On the other side of the border, in the Amritsar camp, Gujral's wife, Pushpa Gujral, had taken the rescued girl, Jaswant Kaur, to work with her. Thousands of girls who had been kidnapped and then rescued were living in the Amritsar camp. Many among them, after a span of few months, started showing signs of pregnancy. Jaswant Kaur was one of them, but at no cost was she ready to leave her mother and go back to Pakistan to live with Ghulam Ishaq again. Her mother agreed and was ready to keep her daughter for the rest of her life despite the pregnancy, but her teenage son, Bhagwan Singh, created a ruckus as he felt that it would bring disgrace to the family. Therefore, he decided they could not live with her anymore. Pushpa Gujral tried to convince Bhagwan Singh and even threatened to expel the family from the refugee camp, but he turned a deaf ear to her threats and one night, both the mother and her son ran away from the camp. Poor Jaswant was left all alone and, finally, Pushpa Gujral decided to provide her with shelter. I spoke to Naresh Gujral, member of Parliament and Gujral's grandson about this matter. He said that there were two more girls who had been disowned by their families because they were raped and became pregnant during Partition, but his grandmother, Pushpa, helped them lead a new life and allowed them to live with her for an indefinite period. She had built Naari Niketan (a house meant to provide shelter and to serve underprivileged women) in Jalandhar. Pushpa Gujral got Jaswant Kaur married and she was happy with her new family. She served as the superintendent of Naari Niketan till her last breath.

Incidents like the one that happened with Jaswant Kaur took place with thousands of women during Partition. Muslim, Hindu and Sikh girls were all subjected to these heinous crimes. Around a million girls were kidnapped overall.[*] In order to bring them back to their families and country, and accommodate them in mainstream society, Nehru and Jinnah signed the Inter Dominion Agreement, 1947. The governments of both the countries appointed highly qualified women who belonged to high-class families to facilitate the task. On the Indian side, Rameshwaran Nehru and Mridula Sarabhai were in charge. Along with Mridula, Kamlaben Patel, a Gandhian woman, was also part of this team. In an interview,

[*] Kamlaben Patel, 'Oranges and Apples', *1947 Lahore*, p. 169.

Kamlaben said that till the year 1952, only 30,000 women out of the million could be found and rescued, out of which 12,000 were Muslim and 18,000 were Sikh and Hindu.

Another such tragic story was narrated to me by my friend Rohit Bal Vohra, who went on to become a senior advisor to Star Network in India. He used to be a leader in the Congress party. Rohit aka Pappu had told me that his family was also based in Lahore and during the Partition riots, his bua (father's sister) was kidnapped. He said that his grandmother loved her daughter very much and after this unfortunate incident, she would miss her and cry day and night and passed her days with just her daughter's memories. After a span of about a year, the grandmother got to know that her daughter had been rescued by the police in Pakistan from a Muslim family and they had asked the Vohra family to take their daughter back. Rohit Bal Vohra was in tears when he narrated this to me. When his father was going to bring his sister back, Vohra's grandmother stopped him at the doorstep and said that Vohra's aunt was no more a part of the family, and so there was no need to bring her back. Vohra said that his father was stunned. But his grandmother was stubborn and was firm in her decision to not to get her daughter back as it would bring disgrace to the family because she had lived with a Pakistani Muslim family.

There are thousands of such stories where the pride of the family overpowered feelings of love and humanity. The obsession with family honour forced people to disown their own daughters, and the daughters, who already must have gone through a lot trauma, suffered further by being spurned by their own flesh and blood.

Coming back to the Gujrals, when the situation deteriorated due to the riots, the Gujral family decided to shift to India. Since Avtar Narain Gujral was a member of Parliament in Pakistan, his membership was transferred to the Indian government. Pushpa Gujral was not at all ready to live in Delhi. Finally, one day, Avtar Narain met Nehru. During those days, a member of Parliament used to only get travel allowance and accommodation. Gujral told Nehru that his family was not ready to shift from Jalandhar and he was unable to sustain the household with the money he received as a member of Parliament. Nehru tried to convince him first, but when Gujral refused to come around, Nehru called up the chief minister of Punjab and requested him to give Avtar Narain Gujral any desired post. The chief minister of Punjab gave him the proposal of becoming a cabinet minister. During those days, a cabinet minister used to get paid only Rs 1200. Apart from that, there were vacancies for judges as well, who were paid Rs 3000 along with other facilities. Since Gujral had been a well-known lawyer throughout his life, he chose to become a judge of a tribunal and settled in Jalandhar. Pushpa used to look after Naari Niketan, and its expenses were met by Gujral. It was the year 1979 when Avtar Narain Gujral passed away and thereafter, his son Inder Kumar Gujral bore the expenses of Naari Niketan. In 1988, Pushpa Gujral too passed away, but Naari Niketan is still operational and is in a much better condition than before. After Inder Kumar Gujral, it is his son, Naresh Gujral, who looks after the organization. I once went to Jalandhar to visit Naari Niketan. A huge and well-maintained building, it has a window with a cradle at its entry near the road. A bell inside the building is attached to the cradle using a rope. Unwed mothers or others who for some unfortunate reason are forced to abandon a child can leave the child in the cradle, which makes the bell inside the building ring, alerting the staff.

I.K. Gujral

Both the sons of Avtar Narain Gujral became very famous. Inder Kumar Gujral entered politics and was helped immensely by Sucheta Kriplani (Indian freedom fighter and politician, and also the first woman chief minister of Uttar Pradesh in India). Later, he developed a very close relationship with Indira

Gandhi as well. Indira made him an MP of the Rajya Sabha and a minister of her cabinet. Later, when they started having conflicts because of Sanjay Gandhi, Gujral was sent to Moscow as the ambassador of India and, eventually, he decided to resign from the Congress. Under the government headed by V.P. Singh, Inder Kumar Gujral served as the foreign minister and later served as the prime minister of India for a brief period of ten months. I used to meet Inder Kumar Gujral frequently, and he would share many tales from his life. While he was studying in Lahore, his friend circle included the famous poet and writer Faiz Ahmad Faiz, Rajendra Singh Bedi, Bhisham Sahni, Sahir Ludhianvi, Ali Sardar Jafri and Krishna Chandar. Inder Gujral did not lose touch with them thereafter. Some of his friends settled in Bombay, and he would often visit them. He spent many days at Kaifi Azmi's place in those days and he got Kaifi Azmi's daughter, Shabana, inducted into the Rajya Sabha as well. According to I.K. Gujral, he studied at Hailey College situated in Lahore. The building of this college had been donated by Sir Ganga Ram, the Indian civil engineer and architect. It was here that Gujral was acquainted with Faiz Ahmad Faiz, who was then a young teacher of English. Under his guidance and company, Gujral studied Urdu poetry. According to him, there was a reasonable age difference between them, but they still became good friends. Later, when Gujral was serving as the ambassador of India in Moscow, Faiz had fallen sick and was also in Moscow for treatment. As a tribute to Faiz, Gujral often used to organize gatherings for people to enjoy Faiz's poetry at Gujral's place in Moscow.

Satish Kumar Gujral

Avtar Narain Gujral's second son, Satish Gujral, had become deaf due to the accident as mentioned before and as a result, he also became mute. But in spite of these disabilities, he was truly a specially-abled person. Through his own effort, he became a renowned painter, sculptor and architect. The painting of Lala Lajpat Rai in the Central Hall of the Indian Parliament is by Satish Gujral. The embassy of Belgium in Delhi has also been designed by him. Satish Gujral had gone to Mexico as a scholar in 1952 to pursue his studies in the field of arts. His friends there included Fidel Castro, who later became the president of Cuba. After completing his studies in arts from Lahore, he also joined the J.J. School of Arts in Bombay for further studies. In this college, he befriended Peelu Modi and Zulfikar Ali Bhutto. Satish Gujral has written in his book *Brush with Life: An Autobiography by Satish Gujral* that Bhutto was very enterprising and talkative. Even though he was a student, he once described the tales of the historic conversation between Jinnah and Bhulabhai Desai in a manner that made one feel that he was present at the meeting himself or as if Jinnah himself talked to him often. Bhulabhai Desai was a congress leader who tried to negotiate a pact with Liaquat Ali Khan of the Muslim League to have Hindu and Muslim representation in the government post-Independence. The objective was to convince the Muslim League leaders to stop their demand for a separate country for Muslims. According to Satish, Bhutto's mother was a Hindu—his mother's maiden name was Lakhi Bai—but he still advocated for the idea of creating a separate country for Muslims.

When Satish Gujral had completed his studies from Bombay's J.J. College, he opened a painting studio on McLeod Road, Lahore, for which his father Avtar Narain Gujral extended financial support from his savings. When the riots had just begun in Lahore, his elder brother Inder Kumar and their mother were in Karachi. Satish thought that these riots were nothing more than a ruckus created by the fringe elements of society and the situation would restore itself to normal after some time. He, therefore, decided not to leave Lahore and continued to operate his studio. Every day, he used to see hundreds of people moving from Lahore with all of their stuff to India and people from east Punjab in India coming to Lahore in an attempt to save their lives, but Satish was least bothered about his own safety. The dense smoke from arson around Lahore was also not enough of a warning sign for him. His house was located near Nishat Cinema in Lahore. Suddenly, one day, his house was attacked by the rioters but, somehow, he managed to run away and succeeded in saving his life. Satish was confused and did not know what to do and where to go, but amidst this difficult situation, he remembered his uncle, Achint Ram. He lived in Lajpat Bhawan and adjacent to it was D.A.V. College Hostel; Achint Ram protected many families. Satish ran a distance of 5 kilometres and reached his place. Achint Ram took good care of Satish. They lived in a place that was being guarded by the Gorkha soldiers, but they always feared that the uncontrollable mob would attack them at any time. After spending quite a few days there, Satish went to his father in Jhelum. His father was working on the task of protecting people on both sides of the border on the orders of Nehru, Jinnah and Liaquat Ali. Inder Kumar was residing in Karachi during those days and was running an export business. Satish managed to safely reach Bombay with his mother and other members of the family on one of the ships of Scindia Shipping Companies.

Beas River Catastrophe

In the state of Punjab, there was another catastrophic incident to which people on both sides of the border fell prey. This incident is referred to as the Beas Catastrophe in Satish Gujral's autobiography. It was an event that clearly displayed nature's anger towards what was being done by the people in the name of Partition. The fury of nature was such that it was adamant on destroying mankind as it saw people destroying one another.

In the month of September in 1947, torrential rains leading to floods were witnessed. This flooded all the five rivers of Punjab;

this was when the evacuation and migration of refugees was at its chaotic peak. People who had left their lives behind and were on the move to find refuge were severely affected by these floods. They had camped at a stretch of road that lay between the River Beas and one of its seasonal tributaries a few miles away.

Pounded by torrential rain and without any shelter over their heads, these tormented souls could not survive the wrath of nature and thousands were drowned in a watery grave by the Beas. For weeks after the incident, the stench of the corpses was said to be unbearable.

Here, it is important to observe that during Partition, one of the groups of people who suffered tremendously were the people of Punjab. This is because they had to either travel by foot or by roads or trains in all these modes, people were being massacred. So, they were in a Catch-22 situation. On the other hand, the Sindhis went to India from Karachi via the sea route, on a ship or a steamer and, therefore, they did not suffer as much. In a similar manner, the Muslims of Gujarat and Maharashtra moved to Pakistan via sea and managed to keep themselves alive. But those who went to Pakistan from east Punjab were mostly killed in the violent clashes.

Kuldip Nayar

Another renowned personality named Kuldip Nayar, the eminent Indian journalist, was based in Sialkot. His father was a dentist. When the city began to witness riots, his father's Muslim friends suggested that he go to Delhi for a few days. Kuldeep told me that one of his father's friends was going to Delhi the same night. His father decided that Kuldeep should immediately leave for Delhi with him. Kuldeep said that he could only take with him the clothes he was wearing and left for Delhi in a jeep. He was unaware of the whereabouts of his family at this point. After facing a lot of difficulties, his parents also managed to reach Delhi. Kuldeep said his mother felt very sad about leaving her home and hoped that they would return to Sialkot someday, but unfortunately, that could never happen. They also had to leave behind many valuables in Sialkot. She missed everything, especially her sarees, sweaters and one-of-a-kind coats and shawls. Kuldeep Nayar struggled a lot in Delhi. At first, he worked for Urdu newspapers and, thereafter, he went to America to pursue his education in the field of journalism. In the US, he even worked as a waiter at a restaurant. Later, when he returned to India, he got a government job and served as the press facilities officer of Lal Bahadur Shastri (the second prime minister of India and a prominent leader during the fight for India's freedom). Kuldeep became one of the most well-known journalists of India. He also served as the member of the Rajya Sabha and as the Indian High Commissioner to London. Jinnah was also interested in appointing Kuldeep's father-in-law, Bhim Sen Sachar, as a minister in Pakistan. Later, he became the chief minister of the state of Punjab in India. Kuldeep's brother-in-law, Rajendra Sachar, was a famous judge. The Sachar committee report related to the status of minorities is very well known. This committee was headed by Rajendra Sachar.

In fact, Kuldeep Nayar and Rajendra Sachar always advised and encouraged me to write a book on Partition. Today, however, they are no longer present amongst us, but I still remember how they used to interrupt me in the middle of our conversations just to ask, 'Rajeev, have you written that book or not?'

Taimur Bande's maternal grandfather, Asgar Khan, and grandmother,
Minni Chowksi

Minni Chowksi from her young days

From left to right: Rajeev Shukla, Khurshid Mahmud Kasuri, Ravi Shankar Prasad, Gautam Singhania and Sunil Shetty in Pakistan, 2004

From left to right: Rajeev Shukla, Jagmohan Dalmia, Arun Jaitley, Priyanka Gandhi Vadra, Rahul Gandhi, Robert Vadra

Ram Lal Anand (Babuji)

Dr G.P. Talwar receiving the Padma Bhushan

Dr G.P. Talwar with Prime Minister Indira Gandhi

Imtiaz Humayun, at 20 years

Imtiaz Humayun with his wife,
Begum Zahur E Fatima

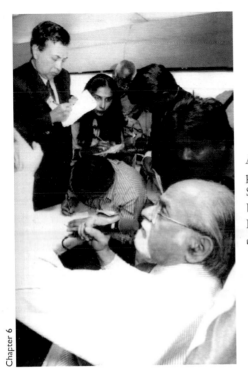

A press conference on the prime minister's plane. Standing left to right: N. Ram (holding a notepad), H.K. Dua (extreme right) and Rajiv Shukla

Champa Tiwari

Gauri Khan with her maternal grandmother, Champa Tiwari

From left to right: Ramesh Chandra Chhibber, Champa Tiwari,
Savita Chhibber, Abram Khan, Shahrukh Khan

Abida Sultan in 1932 before her
wedding in Bhopal

Shahryar Khan in 1948 at Oundle
School in Northampshire, England

Shahryar Khan in Bhopal, India

The three princesses of Bhopal,
1926

A young Abida Sultan

Nawab Sarwar Ali of Kurwai, before his marriage to Abida Sultan, and his family with Mahatma Gandhi

Sarkar Amma with the three princesses of Bhopal

7

Gauri Khan's Grandmother from Lyallpur

The Textile Mills of Faisalabad

The city that is called Faisalabad in Pakistan today was earlier known as Lyallpur. Today, if you travel towards Karachi from Lahore, you will come across Faisalabad just ahead of Sheikhupura district. Here, you will find numerous small textile mills producing high-quality linen. However, an absence of adequate machinery and lack of safety measures for the workers casts a shadow of doubt on the functioning of these mills. When I was on my way to Faisalabad and decided to visit some mills, I got to know that the biggest challenge faced by the workers there was that they ended up inhaling the small particles of cotton they ended up inhaling and which got stuck in their lungs. This is a big health hazard for the workers. When I had a word with the owners of the mill—most of whom are based in Faisalabad (Lyallpur) itself—and asked them what measures they had adopted to ensure the safety of their workers, they replied that they offered them jaggery to eat as it is known to clean the lungs. But other than that, no special medical allowance was given to them.

Shah Rukh Khan's In-Laws

Now you must be thinking why I visited Faisalabad (Lyallpur). A family dear to me, Tiwari–Chibba, is based in Panchsheel Park in Delhi. Tejendra Tiwari's mother, Champa Tiwari, hailed from Lyallpur and the family of Tejendra Tiwari's sister, Savita Chibba, lives with the Tiwaris under one roof. Savita's daughter is Gauri, who is married to the famous Bollywood actor Shah Rukh Khan. Often, when I used to visit Shah Rukh Khan's in-laws with him, I would meet Champa Tiwari, who was Gauri's maternal grandmother. Gauri's family is now Shah Rukh's family and every time he visits Delhi, he stays with them and Gauri's family treats him as their own son. Champa Tiwari used to talk to me about Pakistan often as I visited that country frequently. What I could sense was that though she was based in Delhi, her heart still resided in Lyallpur. I observed that she was happiest when narrating stories related to Lyallpur. She even requested me to take her to Lyallpur. She wanted to see her house, her school, her city and her village, but her children did not want her to travel so far at her age.

Champa Tiwari's husband was Rai Bahadur Sardar Thakar Singh, a Mohyal Brahmin (Mohyal Brahmins are a section of Indian Brahmins with origins in the Punjab region). Thakar Singh's father, Sardar Jawahar Singh, was in the Bengal Lancers division of the British Army. The family owned a lot of land. They had huge tracts of land in Lyallpur too and, moreover, their village was also named after Thakar Singh. Champa used to live in the village adjacent to the city, and her house in the city was in the Vakilaa di Gali (Lawyer's Lane) locality, which was close to the Lyallpur clock tower, situated in the middle of the city. Champa was married to a resident of Lahore, Somdutt Tiwari, who had completed his studies from Government College, Lahore. The Tiwari family shifted to Punjab from Banaras hundreds of years ago and was very rich. They also owned many acres of land in

Toba Tek Singh province, Kartarpur and Himachal Pradesh as well. Somdutt Tiwari's family were considered to be very well educated and were landlords. Somdutt's father Surajbhaan Tiwari, at that time, graduated from St Stephen's College, Delhi, and his grandfather Pundit Kashiram Tiwari was an engineer who graduated from Roorkee Engineering College. After Partition, they were given 150 acres of land each in Anandpur Sahib and Banga against the properties that they held in Pakistan. They had a huge farmhouse in Kartarpur near Jalandhar where they settled after Partition and already owned land in Himachal. Later, Champa Tiwari shifted to Delhi with her son Tejendra and daughter Savita. She passed away in 2018 at the age of ninety-eight; during the Partition, she must have been around twenty-seven. Maybe that is why she remembered each and every moment of her life in Lyallpur. Though the city had been renamed Faisalabad long ago, she still used to call it Lyallpur. I thought that since Champa ji herself could not visit Lyallpur, I could at least get her something from there to refresh her memories attached with that place. When I went to Lahore next, I planned a visit to Lyallpur and informed the deputy commissioner of that place about my arrival. He happened to organize a lunch at the residence of the largest textile mill owner there.

When I reached Lyallpur aka Faisalabad, I found that it was the same old city but with some expansions. New parks and universities had been built, but all the other old structures were intact. The old houses were intact and there were very few that had been either renovated or reconstructed. When I reached Faisalabad, I got in touch with Champa Tiwari over the phone. First, I decided to visit her college and school—Queen Mary's College. Its building was a very old structure that had not been reconstructed. The school building was huge and looked quite grand. The college building was also as it had been long ago, and I clicked many photographs of the school and college. After visiting these places, I made my way towards her house located in Vakilaa di gali. The area was

very crowded and full of mom-and-pop stores. Vakilaa di gali was
actually a lane that had many two- and three-storey houses, but
the difference was that now the place had become very dirty, and
naked electrical wires could be seen everywhere. Moreover, the
houses had not been renovated. Champa's house was such that it
looked like the luxurious residence of a rich and wealthy family.
Looking at the design, arches and the balconies of the house, I
felt that it was quite an exquisite structure. I clicked photographs
of that house as well. Hardly 200 metres away, there was a clock-
tower crossing which was very busy and crowded. Surprisingly,
the new resident of their house had not bothered to get the house
renovated or even giving it a fresh coat of paint.

The Allotment of Properties

In fact, the refugees who came from eastern Punjab were either
allotted houses randomly or they themselves captured whichever
house they found vacant. The houses built and owned by the
Hindus and the Sikhs were huge and luxurious, which poorer
Muslims got an opportunity to capture. However, they were
financially incapable of taking care of these houses. The rules that
were framed read that the Muslims who came to Pakistan from
India to reside permanently would be allotted houses according to
the quality and area of properties held by them in India. In short,
a Muslim emigrant would be allotted a house to live according
to the financial status that they held while they resided in India.
However, this rule was violated to a great extent. People either
bribed the officers or lied to them without producing sufficient
documentation of the properties they had back in India. A
member of the Punjab Legislative Assembly at that time, Jahanara
Shahnawaz, went on to write* that there was so much fraud in the

---

* A. Salim and M. Amruddin, *Lahore 1947*, 2nd ed., Tara Press, 2006,
pp. 257–259.

allotment of houses and plots that the most non-deserving people who migrated to Pakistan from India ended up living in huge bungalows, even though they did not even know how to turn on an electrical switch. Later, the Muslims who were actually rich and had vast properties in pre-Partition India had to live in ordinary houses in Pakistan since the country had run out of appropriate accommodation for them. The Hindus and the Sikhs had huge and luxurious bungalows in Lahore, Rawalpindi, Lyallpur, Jhelum, Gujranwala and Sialkot in Pakistan. But their houses were captured by those who could not have even dreamed to have such houses earlier. For them, Partition proved to be a blessing in disguise. The fault lay with the officers, who were either careless or dishonest, at the rehabilitation department in Pakistan.

On the other hand, the officers on the Indian side of the border treated all the Hindu and Sikh refugees with respect and care. After proper verification of documents and their financial status, the allotment of houses, plots and shops was done without any fraud and partiality. The entire process was monitored by Pandit Jawaharlal Nehru, the first prime minister of India, who personally oversaw the entire matter of property distribution among the people who came from Pakistan.

Champa Tiwari's Lyallpur

Looking at Champa Tiwari's residence, I felt that all the houses in that locality were illegally occupied by those who could not otherwise afford them.

However, after visiting Champa's house, I came to the clock-tower crossing. Clock towers can be found in several small cities of India as well. They are built in the middle of the cities and are tall, steeple-like structures that are very beautiful. They have a clock fitted in them that rings every hour to let the people know the time. If it is 12 o'clock, the clock rings twelve times, and if it is 10 o'clock, it rings ten times and so on. This is how the people of the city come to know the time. When I was there, I saw a lot of hustle and bustle at Lyallpur's clock-tower crossing. There were shops and stores all around. But I was astonished to see that no changes had been made at all to the clock tower. It was made with marble all around, with Sanskrit verses written on it. There were Vedic mantras engraved on it along with the prayer songs for Lord Shiva, Lord Rama and Lord Krishna. Neither the government nor the people of Faisalabad demanded that the carvings be removed. I felt very happy to see Sanskrit shlokas engraved on a monument in Faisalabad. Moving on, around 500 metres away, there was a temple of Lord Shiva, which was intact and in its original form. Nobody had demolished that temple, and a few metres ahead, there was a temple of Lord Rama, again in its original form, the white dome of which was clearly visible from a distance. The only difference was that there was nobody to worship at these temples and their doors were locked. However, nobody was allowed to demolish these sacred structures. The roads and localities which were named after Hindu gods and goddesses had not been renamed. Only the city was renamed as Faisalabad. I also went to have a look at the railway station from where Champa Tiwari always boarded the train for Lahore.

The interesting part was that when I was standing at the clock-tower crossing, I was talking to Champa ji over the phone, and it was she who asked me if there was a Shiv temple ahead. Then she asked me if the Ram Janki temple was still located at so-and-so place. I followed her directions over the phone and described to her whatever I saw on the way. Suddenly, she said that there was a kulfi vendor who would be stationed in a corner of the clock tower which she would visit frequently. It was on the southern corner of the clock tower. I looked around for the kulfi vendor for quite some time and finally spotted him! I went to his shop to eat a kulfi and asked the owner, who was an aged Muslim man, 'How long have you been running this shop?' He replied that it had been more than eighty years that he had been selling kulfis there.

He and his father had not made any changes to the shop, and they still sold kulfi-faluda the same way they both used to eighty years ago. When I asked him about Partition, he replied that he was a young man and used to help his father in the shop. 'We used to serve many customers at that time and earn huge profits', he said. I asked him, 'Why is it that you used to earn more before the Partition as compared to now?' He said that earlier rich and affluent seths and lalas used to live there and were his customers, as they were very fond of his kulfi. He said that there would be a crowd of Sikhs and Hindus before Partition who would eat a lot and were ready to shell out a good amount of money. 'Now the place has become home to a bunch of penniless people who neither have enough money nor sentiments. That is why, now, I do not add exotic or expensive items to the kulfi like fruits and syrup as I used to,' he said. When I told him that I had come from Delhi and was on the phone with the daughter of Thakar Singh, he was shocked. He said that he knew the family since his childhood and used to send kulfi to them almost every day. 'They used to reside in a house in the previous lane from here', he said. He was very happy to learn that Thakar Singh's daughter was still alive. He insisted on not charging me for the kulfi, saying that I was his guest. While I was leaving, he said that though the name of this city has been changed to Faisalabad, the *faisla* (decision) of Partition was not good.

When I returned to Delhi, I gave all the photographs that I had clicked to Champa Tiwari. She jumped in excitement looking at them. I also shared all my experiences of the visit with her, and she listened to them very carefully. Her dream of going to Lyallpur could not be fulfilled, but she felt content just looking at the photographs and listening to my descriptions. During the Partition, she was in Dalhousie, where she owned a house. Earlier there were rumours that Dalhousie may also be merged with Pakistan, but eventually, it became an integral part of India, and therefore, Champa ji did not need to go anywhere. However, her husband, Somdutt Tiwari, was stuck in Lahore. His residence in Lahore was attacked and looted by rioters as he hid inside an almirah for hours. The attackers could not find him though. Later, the Gorkha soldiers arrived at the residence and their firing scared the attackers away. These soldiers rescued Tiwari and helped him reach India.

The Wealthiest Industrialist of Faisalabad

When I was in Faisalabad, the deputy commissioner had organized a lunch for me at the residence of the wealthiest industrialist of that city. I was warmly welcomed and the dining table was full of vegetarian food. Different types of vegetables, dals, salads and fruits were prepared. Both the young industrialist brothers were serving as great hosts, when suddenly an aged person, who must have been about eighty years old, came to hug me. He sat at the dining table and said that the industrialists were his sons, who had told him that a guest from India was coming to the house, and he was eager to meet me. 'I knew that you eat vegetarian food, so I went with my driver myself to buy different vegetables in the morning and told my chef how to cook the Indian vegetables and dals', he said.

He was very excited and had a gregarious personality. He said that whenever he met an Indian, he felt like he was sitting with another member of his family. His fondness for his childhood home and city was evident when he spoke to me: 'I am from Jalandhar. During the Partition, I was studying in school. In my memories, Jalandhar, even today, is still as fresh from when I left the city. I was so familiar with my city that even if you leave me anywhere today, I can navigate to my childhood home easily. Even after sixty-eight years, I am sure I have not forgotten even a single place in Jalandhar, but, unfortunately, I could not go to there ever again.'

Madan Lal Khurana

I recall another tale about Lyallpur. The former chief minister of Delhi, Madan Lal Khurana, also hailed from Lyallpur and, till the end, he felt proud of having been a resident of that place. In the year 1947, he was just eleven years old when violent riots hit the city. He was made to stay in a camp of D.A.V. School where many refugees were living. The Hindus and Sikhs had formed their own groups and so had the Muslims. The members of both groups used to attack and vandalize each other's houses, and one day, the D.A.V. School camp was also attacked. Finally, it was decided that all the refugees would be taken to Amritsar on a train. The train driver was intentionally stopping in the jungles, and it seemed as if he wanted the passengers to be attacked. When the train reached Lahore, he stopped it again and, consequently, the rioters started firing bullets from both sides. Although there were Gorkha soldiers deployed for the protection of passengers, they were finding it difficult to face the bullets. Finally, one of the soldiers dared to step out and somehow reached the engine room. He pointed his pistol at the driver and threatened to kill him if he did not start the train. Scared, the driver agreed to move again. When the railway officials got to know that the train towards Amritsar was being attacked at many places, they decided to change its destination to Ferozepur via Kasur city. After becoming a union minister, Khurana would recall how his life and that of his co-passengers was saved by a Gorkha soldier. Had the soldier not pointed his pistol at the driver, all the passengers would probably have been killed in a massacre. Khurana said that his family members never imagined that they would have to leave Lyallpur forever in this manner. Hence, apart from some necessary items, everything was left behind. He said that most of the Hindus and Sikhs believed that even if Pakistan came into existence, they would not have to leave their native land and would continue to live there peacefully. They never believed that they would be forced to leave the place where their ancestors had been living for hundreds of years. All these people had no objection to continue living in Pakistan, but the violence of the riots and bloody massacres forced them to leave their homes overnight.

While returning from Lyallpur, I came to know that Nankana Sahib, the birthplace of the first Sikh guru, Guru Nanak Dev, was nearby. I went there and bowed my head to the floor in obeisance. The Sikhs have also made a colony there. When I reached, all the Sikhs gathered around me and said that they faced a lot of difficulties and were made to run from pillar to post whenever they applied for the Indian visa. I later conveyed their message to the then prime minister of India Manmohan Singh, who passed the necessary orders in this regard.

The city of Lyallpur is still fresh in my memory. The specialty of this place is its fertile agricultural land. All of this used to be owned by Hindu and Sikh landlords and the Muslims used to work as labourers.

Mehmood Haq Alvi

I was also reminded me of another elderly person named Mehmood Haq Alvi. I once visited Islamabad to attend a conference of the South Asia Free Media Association (SAFMA). I was serving as a member of Parliament at that time, and the association had also invited MP-cum-journalists like me and Kuldeep Nayyar. Among the politicians, Lalu Prasad Yadav and Ram Vilas Paswan were there. We were all put up at the Marriott Hotel. This dates back to the year 2003 when the Mariott was considered the best hotel in Islamabad. Unfortunately, some terrorists have now destroyed the beautiful property by bombing it. Lalu Prasad Yadav was very popular among the people of Pakistan and whenever I took him along to the markets of Rawalpindi and Islamabad, he would be surrounded by crowds. I remember that Sheikh Rasheed Ahmad, who was the Information and Broadcasting minister of Pakistan from 2002 to 2004 and is currently serving as the interior minister, residing in Rawalpindi, had taken him to his home and told the media that if Lalu Prasad Yadav contested elections from there, he would enjoy a landslide victory.

Moving on, I used to exercise daily in the gymnasium at the Marriott. One day, the manager came to me and said, 'Alvi Sahab wants to meet you.' I asked him, 'Who is he?' He replied that he was one of the well-known builders of Islamabad and that half the city had been constructed by him. He said that Alvi Sahab has been saying that his relative has come from India and he wants to meet him. When I asked him who he was referring to, he said that Alvi has a habit of calling every Indian his relative and has great respect for Indians. I agreed to meet him the next day. Alvi was waiting for me in the health club. He must have been about seventy-five years old and used to come to the health club for exercise daily. The moment I approached him, he hugged me and said that he was eagerly waiting for me. As we began talking, he told me that he saw me on TV often and that he considered all Indians very close to his heart. He told me he used to live in Karol Bagh in Delhi, which is where he had studied. 'Even today, I see Karol Bagh in my dreams. I have not forgotten anything. I also remember the Gayatri mantra', he said and thereafter started chanting it with perfect pronunciation. He then started reciting the *stuti* (a form of prayer) of Lord Shiva in Sanskrit. I was stunned to see him crying. I tried to console him. He said that after Partition, he moved to Rawalpindi and started construction work and now, with the blessings of Allah, the enterprise had transformed into a huge company. Alvi then invited me to his place for a meal. But the prime minister of Pakistan had invited me, Lalu Prasad Yadav and another member of Parliament, Prem Gupta, for dinner at his residence the same day. Since Alvi sahab was adamant about his invitation, I took him to Lalu Yadav. At first instance, Yadav was a bit angry. But when I told him everything, he also became emotional. Alvi recited Sanskrit shlokas in front of Yadav as well.

Yadav told him that we had to ensure our presence at the prime
minister's residence for dinner, but Alvi suggested that we could
perform all the formalities there and then have our dinner at his
place. We agreed. He then said that he will send his cars to pick us
all from the prime minister's residence. When we were hurriedly
finishing our food at the PM's house, the PM asked us if we
had somewhere to go after the dinner. I told him that there was
someone called Mehmood Haq Alvi, an old man and a builder
in Islamabad by profession, who had invited us home. To my
surprise, the PM knew who he was and insisted that we must visit
his place. Soon, the cars arrived to pick us up.

When we came out, we saw three cars—a Rolls Royce,
Mercedes and a BMW lined up. They took us to a luxurious marble
bungalow in sector G-7. As a token of respect, Alvi had thrown a
party for us. The former president Ayub Khan's son, Gohar Ayub
Khan, relatives of another former president Yahiya Khan (martial
administrator and president of Pakistan) along with other ministers
and officers of Pakistan were present there. Alvi Sahab treated us to
sumptuous food and all the guests were eager to click photographs
with Lalu Prasad Yadav. A young female member of Parliament,
Kashmala Tariq, was also present amidst us.

On this visit to Pakistan, we were invited by General Musharraf
to the President's House for tea. In this meeting, Ram Vilas Paswan
introduced himself to General Musharraf saying he had resigned
from his post during the regime of Atal Bihari Vajpayee following
the Gujarat riots for the way the then government handled the
issue. This became a big media controversy, after which he severed
ties with the NDA government too.

On my journey to Islamabad, Ashwini Minna aka Ashwini
Kumar Chopra, a senior journalist, resident editor of the *Punjab
Kesari* and a Lok Sabha member in India, accompanied me till
Peshawar. We visited the old localities of Peshawar as well. On
the way to Peshawar comes the city of Attock. At that time,
Peshawar was a very peaceful place though now it has become

a hub of terrorists. We saw gun cartridges being sold openly like potatoes and onions in the markets there. A team of journalists was taken to Pakistan-occupied-Kashmir (PoK) as well, but the Indian High Commissioner had directed me and Kuldeep Nayar not to visit PoK since we were members of Parliament. So we returned after visiting the Murree hill station.

Alvi Sahab remained in touch with me for many years after this trip, and whenever I would send someone from India to Islamabad, he took good care of them.

8

Pakistan

Jinnah's Unfulfilled Dream

Whenever I visit Pakistan, I always end up wondering whether it is the same Pakistan that Muhammad Ali Jinnah dreamt of.

Jinnah was a Khoja (*Khwaja*) Muslim.* The community's demarcation with Hindus was rather fluid in view of the similarity in customs and traditions. Jinnah received a Western education that had a major influence on his lifestyle and thought process. In his formative years, he did not believe in the idea of a religion-based division of people.

He learnt and practised law in London but soon set up his practice in Bombay and established himself as a highly regarded lawyer. His cases were featured in prominent newspapers time and again. Once in the public eye, Jinnah decided to join politics. In 1905, Jinnah became vocal about his political stance opposing the British government. During this time, the All India Muslim League was also being formed and gaining steam under the aegis of Sir

---

* The Khojas are a mainly Nizari Isma'ili Shia community of people originating in India. They are historically members of the Bania caste.

Aga Khan. The League enjoyed British support as the foreigners wanted to use the League as an instrument to counterbalance the influence of Hindus on the overall demographics of the Indian subcontinent. At that time, Jinnah voiced his stance against the government's attempt to create a rift between Hindus and Muslims. He termed it an imperial ploy to destroy the harmony between the two religions in the country.

Jinnah's social standing in the elite circles of Bombay brought him in touch with a young Parsi girl named Rattanbai Petit, famously known as Ruttie, who was the daughter of Sir Dinshaw Petit, a notable social and political figure of the time. For her, Jinnah was not like any other Muslim man. In her view, he was progressive in his ideology with a Western outlook and a nationalist bent of mind. She saw him as a perfect companion for herself. For Jinnah too, she was the perfect modern Parsi woman. In 1918, Rattanbai turned eighteen and they got married at Jinnah's house in Bombay as per Shia Islamic law. Ruttie converted to Shia Islam as a mere formality because of the requirements of Sharia law and not because Jinnah had placed any such condition.

After 1927, Jinnah was mostly away from India. In 1929, his wife passed away, following which he started practising law in London again. In 1934, he was persuaded by his supporters to return to India as the Muslim League had grown substantially by then, and Jinnah had a good chance of relaunching his political career.

It needs to be noted that when in 1905 Jinnah had been ignored by Muslim political leaders due to his secular ideology, he flew back to London and started practising law there. But when he returned from London in 1934, his words proved that his new views were in contradiction to his earlier ones. Jinnah now had a better chance of advocating for a separate country for Muslims, of which he could be the head. He soon became one of the most active and prominent leaders of the Muslim League.

Louis Fischer at 10, Aurangzeb Road

When Mahatma Gandhi tried to explain to him the repercussions of his demand, Jinnah declared Gandhi a leader of the Hindus and alleged that the Congress too had vested interests in the well-being of only Hindus. Gandhi asked Louis Fischer, an American journalist close to him, to convince Jinnah to refrain from what he was doing. Fischer visited Jinnah's then home in Delhi, which at that time was at 10, Aurangzeb Road, which now happens to be the residence of the ambassador of the Netherlands.

Here, I will digress a little to share an interesting anecdote about this house. The government of the Netherlands has maintained the house in its original style and has also got a booklet published that depicts the room in which Gandhi used to meet Jinnah, where Nehru would sit when he would visit Jinnah, and so on. Ramkrishna Dalmia, the founder of Dalmia Group (which is a big conglomerate that owned Bennett Coleman & Co., publishers of the *Times of India*), was Jinnah's best friend and visited his place almost every evening. Jinnah had purchased the house from Dalmia for a sum of Rs 3 lakhs. But when Jinnah was leaving for Pakistan after Partition, the price of the property had skyrocketed. Out of respect and the deep bond of friendship that existed between the two, Jinnah decided to sell the house back to Dalmia for exactly the amount he had paid to purchase it. Dalmia later sold the house to the Netherlands government. It is a beautiful bungalow spread across many acres of land.

Coming back to journalist Louis Fischer, when he went to meet Jinnah in this house on Gandhi's request, Fischer got late for their meeting as the taxi that he had hired broke down on its way. Meanwhile, Jinnah was angrily pacing in the lawn of his house and it was only after Fischer was given an earful about his late arrival that the discussion began. Fischer has written in his memoir that he put forth the proposal made by Gandhi to Jinnah, which was that if Jinnah wanted to be the first prime minister of India, he could be, but at no cost should the country be divided on religious lines. Listening to this, Jinnah raised his head in frustration and anger and asked Fischer to go and tell Gandhi that he just wanted a separate nation and would accept nothing less than that.

Birla House

Disappointed, Fischer walked back to Birla House, which was just 500 metres away. Nowadays, it is located adjacent to the Claridge's Hotel at the Tees January Marg. When Fischer conveyed Jinnah's response to Gandhi, he too was disappointed. Gandhi is reported to have said angrily that it seemed Jinnah had gone mad, and from that day, Gandhi gave up the hope of saving the nation from being partitioned. Gandhi used to stay at Birla House, and it was there that he was shot dead on 30 January 1948. Later, in order to convert the place into a memorial for Gandhi, the government took over that house from Ghanshyam Das Birla who had built it, and in exchange, gave him a plot located adjacent to it. According to the freedom fighter Shashi Bhushan, the government also gave him a sum of approximately Rs 50 lakh. Birla had built his own bungalow on the government-allotted plot where Birla's son, Krishna Kumar Birla, lived till his last breath. This house is still owned by the Birla family. However, Birla House was a huge bungalow and the plot given in exchange for that house was comparatively smaller in size.

After the meeting between Louis Fischer and Jinnah, Nehru and Patel met Viceroy Mountbatten to begin the formal discussion about the Partition.

The Fight for Ferozepur

For Partition, Lord Mountbatten appointed Sir Cyril Radcliffe, a prominent lawyer in England, as the chairman of the boundary commission. Sir Radcliffe had lived in Moscow for some time but had never visited India before. However, that did not prevent him from serving as the chairman for both Punjab and Bengal. The viceroy had decided that in case of any conflict, the final decision of Sir Radcliffe would prevail.

In the Punjab Boundary Commission, advocate Sir Mohammad Zafarullah Khan was contesting on behalf of the Muslims; he later became the first foreign minister of Pakistan. On the other hand, M.C. Setalvad, the then attorney general, who lived in Bombay and used to travel to Lahore, was appointed to represent the Indian side and was assisted by Bakshi Tek Chand, retired judge of Lahore High Court, who was a well-known lawyer at the Lahore Bar. Justice Deen Mohammad and Justice Mohammad Munir were among the Muslim members of the Punjab Boundary Commission. Justice Mehar Chand Mahajan and Justice Teja Singh were among the Hindu and Sikh members. Jinnah had appointed as the advocate of the Muslims Zafarullah Khan, who was in Delhi during those days and would visit Lahore for the commission hearings.

According to Zafarullah, one day, Justice Deen Mohammad came nervously to him in the evening. He said that Radcliffe would be conducting a survey alone from a small aircraft the next day. He was concerned that the commission would not come to know what he saw from the aircraft. When Deen Mohammad spoke to him about this, Radcliffe said that there were only three seats on the aircraft and finally agreed to take along one person from each side. Hence, it was decided that Justice Munir and Justice Teja Singh would accompany Radcliffe on the survey.

The very next day, everyone reached Walton Airport in Lahore. But the aerial survey had to be cancelled because of a storm. When Justice Munir asked the pilot where they were supposed to fly, the pilot took out a small piece of paper from his pocket and gave it to him. He was instructed to fly to all the locations mentioned on the paper. They were to first go to Pathankot, where the River Ravi originates, and following the same route, they had to reach

Ferozpur. Justice Munir had a strong suspicion that this might be the borderline for the Partition and that Pakistan would get only a portion of Punjab. Munir was very angry and wanted to leave immediately for Delhi and meet Jinnah to resign from the commission on the ground that everything was pre-decided.

Zafarullah told him that Jinnah would not rely on information that was garnered from only a piece of paper, and that Jinnah would never let him resign from the commission. The very next day, Jinnah came to Lahore and that is what happened. He said that Radcliffe was a good and honest person and would never cheat them; Jinnah reiterated that he had complete faith in him. According to Zafarullah, though Jinnah had appointed him to contest the case as an advocate, none of the leaders of the Muslim League were prepared with any valid document supporting their claim.

In fact, Zafarullah had asked for two stenographers, a pencil, paper and a typewriter from the then chief minister, the Nawab of Mamdot. To his surprise, the Nawab could not even arrange that. He then requested Khwaja Abdul Rahim, who was serving as the commissioner in Rawalpindi. He helped Zafarullah set up a camp office in Lahore with those basic provisions. Zafarullah was appointed as the Muslim League representative in the boundary commission. When the hearings of the commission began, the Muslim League's main contention came down to the following points: They wanted Gurdaspur, Ferozpur and some subdivisions of Jalandhar and Amritsar but the advocate on the Indian side, M.C. Setalvad, was opposing it. The Muslim League's argument was that since the partition was being done on the basis of where the Muslim population was concentrated, these sections of the state should be a part of Pakistan. Their claims included Ferozepur district, Gurdaspur district, Nakodar tehsil of Hoshiarpur, Jeera tehsil, Kapurthala, Kangra district and Ajnala tehsil of Amritsar.

The arguments put forth by them based on the population were so strong and convincing that they thought they would easily

get sixteen districts of Punjab, including these areas. Batala and
Shankargarh along with a few places in the tehsil of Gurdaspur
were already dominantly occupied by Muslims. Sir Cyril Radcliffe
had indicated to the members of the commission in Shimla that
he could not pass any judgement regarding Gurdaspur yet, but
confirmed that Ferozepur would be a part of Pakistan. According
to Zafarullah, a few days after that, the governor of West Punjab,
Evan Meredith Jenkins, received a message from the secretary of
the viceroy, George Abell, that the documents of the Partition
were ready and within forty-eight hours the Partition would be
officially announced; Jenkins was requested to put the police chief
on high alert. A similar kind of message was sent to the governor
of East Punjab, Sir Chandulal Madhavlal Trivedi, and everyone
kept waiting. The official announcement was supposed to be made
in forty-eight hours, but ten days passed and nothing happened.

According to Zafarullah, Pakistan had no recognized
government then. But an interim government, whose prime
minister was Jawaharlal Nehru, did exist, and both the governors
(of East Punjab in India and West Punjab in Pakistan) reported
to him. It seemed as if the authorities had disclosed the proposal
of Partition to Nehru and it felt like a speculation to many
that he conspired to get all those districts that could have been
merged with Pakistan to India, sending Pakistan into a state of
shock. Zafarullah believed that Nehru and Mountbatten were
good friends and Nehru was able to reap the benefits of this
friendship. According to Zafarullah, the headworks of the Sutlej
river canal system were in Ferozepur, which effectively meant
the water supply was controlled from there. These waters used to
flow to Pakistan, Bikaner and Jaisalmer for irrigation purposes,
because of which farming could be carried out in these areas.
Bikaner and Jaisalmer's Rajputana rulers wanted to merge with
Pakistan instead of staying with India, but when Nehru took away
Ferozepur, it turned out to be a double whammy for Pakistan.
The kings of Bikaner and Jaisalmer were now worried that their

water supply would be stopped as Ferozepur was now a part of India, and so they changed their minds and decided to be a part of India. Zafarullah has written in his memoir that it was obvious that Nehru had completely changed the report of the boundary commission in India's favour.

Here, it is important to highlight that not only Zafarullah, but according to British writers Dominique Lapierre and Larry Collins*—who had close ties to Mountbatten—when Radcliffe had submitted the report to the viceroy, Ferozepur and Gurdaspur were part of Pakistan.

The viceroy's secretary, George Abell, was on good terms with Nehru, to whom he allegedly leaked all the information. Nehru complained to Mountbatten. Since Nehru was a very good friend of Mountbatten and his wife, the viceroy told Nehru that he may sit with his (Mountbatten's) stenographer that night and make all the necessary modifications he wanted. And so, Nehru dismissed Pakistan's claims to Gurdaspur, Ferozepur, all the Muslim-dominated tehsils of Amritsar, Kapurthala, Kangra and Hoshiarpur and merged them with India.

Nehru had modified the report of the commission in such a way that Pakistan would be receiving water from only those rivers which were originating from India, making it possible for India to stop the supply of water to Pakistan at any point of time. Also, the sea boundary near Karachi was demarcated in such a way that no ship could reach the seaports of Pakistan without passing through India's territorial waters. Pakistan was tied from all sides.

Pakistan was deeply shocked to learn of this. Zafarullah's words find confirmation in Pakistan's response to the official announcement of Partition—instead of joy and happiness, Pakistan had fallen into a deep state of shock and sadness. A leader of the Muslim League, a close friend of Jinnah's and a former

---

* Dominique Lapierre and Larry Collins, *Freedom at Midnight*, USA: Simon & Schuster, 1975.

member of Parliament, Jahanara Shahnawaz, has written in her memoir about the time when Jinnah was being sworn in at the Governor House at Karachi; she said there was an environment of complete sadness and nobody was happy. The fact that Ferozepur and Gurdaspur could not be part of the territories of Pakistan was the main reason behind the country's grief. Jinnah was not happy with Mountbatten at all. The swearing-in ceremony, for which Mountbatten was also present, was carried out by Jahanara's uncle, Chief Justice Mian Abdur Rashid.

Mountbatten was informed by intelligence authorities that due to the perceived injustice done to Pakistan in the allocation of regions and resources, there was a strong chance of an attempt at assassinating him during a planned open-car procession in Karachi to announce the birth of Pakistan. Mountbatten was very sceptical of the welcome he would get in Pakistan and was afraid of going into the procession with Jinnah, but nothing untoward happened during the entire ceremony where Jinnah was appointed as the governor-general of Pakistan.

Zafarullah has also said in his memoir that if Gurdaspur had been made a part of Pakistan, India would have been left with only one way to reach Kashmir, which was via Hoshiarpur, and the Pathan attackers could easily capture Kashmir. The route to Hoshiarpur would have taken years to make since it was a mountainous and uneven terrain with rivers. It would not be easy to make one's way through Hoshiarpur.

This incident is also depicted in a film titled *Jinnah* which was produced in Pakistan fifteen years ago but was not released in India. Well-known journalist Barkha Dutt and I visited Islamabad on a journalistic endeavour. There, we watched this film in a movie theatre. The film tried to portray Nehru as a wicked person who, very cleverly, deceived Pakistan. He was accused of having an affair with Mountbatten's wife, Edwina, with whose help he influenced the viceroy and altered the actual report used for Partition. In the film, Nehru was shown holding Edwina's hand and sitting alone with her. While Jinnah was shown as an honest person and a man of principles, Nehru was portrayed as a trickster. The film was not well-rounded and appeared almost farcical.

As per Zafarullah, immediately after the official announcement of Partition, India stopped the supply of the waters of River Sutlej and River Ravi to Pakistan, which had been Pakistan's biggest fear, that they would starve due to droughts. On 4 May 1948, an agreement was signed according to which, until Pakistan developed its own sources of water, India would continue to supply water to Pakistan and gradually reduce the quantum and, in exchange, Pakistan would have to deposit money in India's State Bank. Later, the World Bank intervened and decided that the waters of the Indian side of Punjab would be used by India and that of Pakistan's side would be used by Pakistan and the organization would sponsor the irrigation system in Pakistan. However, India backed out and did not contribute to the irrigation system of Pakistan. But America, Britain and Australia, along with the World Bank, stepped forward to fund the irrigation needs of Pakistan. However, Pakistan's farming and agriculture would always suffer due to the unfair way in which the Partition was done, as per Zafarullah.

Jinnah dreamt about a Pakistan where Muslims would have a dominant presence and authority in the government, but the non-Muslim people would be given equal rights. Minar-e-Pakistan is a monument near the Lahore Fort where, during a conference of the Muslim League in 1940, the first official call for a separate and independent homeland for the Muslims of British India was made. In the proposal that ratified it, it was clearly written that Hindus, Sikhs and Christians along with people having faith in other religions would not face any kind of discrimination. They would also have complete ownership of the properties and the government would not mete out to them any stepmotherly treatment. The quote from 'Lahore Resolution of 1940' reads: 'Sufficient arrangements will be made to ensure that in the constitution of the new country, special provisions will be made to ensure that the Religious, Cultural, Economic, Political, Administrative rights of the minorities will be completely protected and the advice of the minorities will be considered in the matters pertaining to framing of such provisions in the constitution.' The proposal further stated, 'Similarly, we expect that the Muslims living in India will also be granted the same kind of rights in accordance with this proposal.' Later, on 9 April 1946, in the conference of the Muslim League held in Delhi headed by Jinnah, the provision of equal rights was reiterated in the resolution and was passed. The MLAs of the Muslim League and the members of the provincial assembly were also present in this conference.

The proposal that was ratified in 1940 in Lahore is engraved on a stone wall in Minar-e-Pakistan. It is a monument that has been built in memory of the formation of the country; however, none of the prime ministers of India have ever visited the place as none of them wanted to endorse the fact that Partition was a good decision. Later, when Atal Bihari Vajpayee travelled in the Delhi–Lahore bus to Lahore as the prime minister, he paid a visit to Minar-e-Pakistan with Nawaz Sharif and by signing the visitor's book there, he, in a way, recognized Pakistan as a separate nation in its own right. I had also gone to Lahore during this visit. I saw that the Pakistani media reported the event to say as if India had finally accepted Pakistan and India's prime minister had confirmed this by visiting Minar-e-Pakistan. Nawaz Sharif had taken Vajpayee to the top of the minar in a lift from where one could enjoy the view of the entire city of Lahore, the grand fort and River Ravi. In my opinion, Vajpayee did the right thing by going on this visit as Pakistan is a well-established nation.

From the Lahore resolution of the Muslim League from 1940, it appears that Jinnah envisioned the formation of the new country in a manner that people would not have to leave their hometowns and travel to the other side of the border in search of a place to live. People would continue to live where they were already residing and their fundamental rights would be maintained and protected through and after this transition. Jinnah seems to have thought that the partition of the nation would happen in a very peaceful and decent manner without any violence or riots. He perhaps envisioned India and Pakistan to have relations like the United States of America and Canada. But what happened was just the opposite.

Jinnah said he wanted all Hindus, Sikhs, Christians and Parsis to live in Pakistan. After becoming the governor-general, he referred to this point in his speech in the National Assembly in Karachi, that he wished to protect and maintain all the rights of the minorities in Pakistan. In this momentous speech in 1947, he laid out a clear foundation on which he wanted Pakistan to be built. He mentions the fundamental principles of governance in his speech, some of which are reproduced below:

(1) . . . *the first duty of a government is to maintain law and order, so that the life, property and religious beliefs of its subjects are fully protected by the State.*

(2) *One of the biggest curses . . . is bribery and corruption. That really is a poison. We must put that down with an iron hand.*

(3) . . . *the evil of nepotism and jobbery* [the practice of using a public office or position of trust for one's own gain] . . . *I want to make it quite clear that I shall never tolerate any kind of jobbery, nepotism, or any influence directly or indirectly brought to bear upon me. Whenever I will find that such a practice is in vogue or is continuing anywhere, low or high, I shall certainly not countenance it.*

(4) *I know there are people who do not quite agree with the division of India and the partition of the Punjab and Bengal. But now that it has been accepted, it is the duty of every one of us to loyally abide by it and honourably act according to the agreement which is now final and binding on all.*

(5) *Now if we want to make this great State of Pakistan happy*
and prosperous, we should wholly and solely concentrate on the
well-being of the people, and especially of the masses and the poor.

If you will work in cooperation, forgetting the past, burying
the hatchet, you are bound to succeed. If you change your past and
work together in a spirit that every one of you, no matter to what
community he belongs, no matter what relations he had with you
in the past, no matter what is his colour, caste or creed, is first,
second, and last a citizen of this state with equal rights, privileges
and obligations, there will be no end to the progress you will make.

I cannot emphasize it too much. We should begin to work
in that spirit and in course of time all these angularities of the
majority and minority communities, the Hindu Community and
the Muslim Community—because even as regards Muslims you
have Pathans, Punjabis, Shias, Sunnis, and so on, and among the
Hindus you have Brahmins, Vashnavas, Khatris, also Bengalees,
Madrasis, and so on—will vanish.

Also, he articulated the notion of Pakistani nationalism that
combined religious freedom, political equality and the State's
detachment from religious and sectarian squabbles. He added this
with emphasis:

You are free; you are free to go to your temples, you are free to go
to your mosques, or to any other place of worship in this State of
Pakistan . . . You may belong to any religion or caste or creed—
that has nothing to do with the business of the State . . . We are
starting in the days when there is no discrimination, no distinction
between one caste or creed and another. We are starting with this
fundamental principle of England in course of time had to face the
realities of the situation and had to discharge the responsibilities
and burdens placed upon them by the government ... Today, you
might say with justice that Roman Catholics and Protestants do

not exist; what exists now is that every man is a citizen, an equal citizen of Great Britain ... all members of the Nation.

Finally, he carried the logic of his reasoning to an ultimate and inescapable conclusion, which is the majesty of modern and liberal Islam:

Now I think we should keep in front of us as our ideal and you will find that in course of time Hindus would cease to be Hindus and Muslims would cease to be Muslims, not in the religious sense, because that is the personal faith of each individual, but in the political sense as citizens of the State ... I shall always be guided by the principles of justice and fair play without any, as is put in the political language, prejudice or ill will; in other words, partiality or favouritism. My guiding principle will be justice and complete impartiality, and I am sure that with your support and cooperation, I can look forward to Pakistan becoming one of the greatest Nations of the world.

When L.K. Advani, the veteran Bharatiya Janata Party (BJP) leader, was on a tour in Pakistan, standing before Jinnah's tomb, Advani described the founder of Pakistan as 'secular' and an 'ambassador of Hindu–Muslim unity' for which he was opposed and criticized in India. Even the leaders of the BJP had opposed it; however, I feel he did not say anything wrong.

9

Liaquat Ali Khan and Fatima Jinnah
The Clash of Titans

Here is the story of a person who was the most powerful leader in the Muslim League after Muhammad Ali Jinnah and went on to become the first prime minister of Pakistan. In fact, it was he and his wife Sheila Pant, aka Ra'ana Liaquat, who persuaded Jinnah to return to India from London in 1934 to lead the movement for the formation of Pakistan. We are talking about Liaquat Ali Khan.

While Jinnah is accredited with the creation of Pakistan, it was Liaquat Ali Khan, Begum Liaquat and Fatima Jinnah who provided him with the support he needed.

Liaquat Ali Khan

Liaquat Ali Khan's family was originally Hindu; they belonged to the Jaat caste and hailed from Karnal in Haryana. They had later converted to Islam. His father, Nawab Rustam Ali Khan, was a Nausherwani Marhal landlord who owned 300 villages stretching from Karnal (an erstwhile part of the Punjab province in undivided India) to Muzaffarnagar in Uttar Pradesh, India. He had a huge house and a farmhouse spread over 72 acres of land in the Jansath town of Muzaffarnagar; this house he wanted to sell to his friend, a Congress leader, Rajendra Dutt Tyagi, before he left for Pakistan during Partition. When Tyagi refused to buy it, Liaquat decided to sell the farmhouse to a local businessman.

Liaquat Ali graduated from Aligarh Muslim University, one of the premier institutes of the times situated in Aligarh in Uttar Pradesh, after attaining a degree in law. The he went to the University of Oxford in England to pursue a postgraduate degree in law. In 1931, when he visited Indraprastha College, Delhi, to deliver a speech in a seminar, he met Sheila Pant, a highly educated woman and an upper-class Brahmin. She was from Almora and had a postgraduate degree in economics from Lucknow and had a masters in sociology. She was serving as a professor of economics in Indraprastha College. Eventually, they fell in love and got married. Sheila renamed herself Begum Ra'ana Liaquat and became one of the most active leaders of the Muslim League and worked closely with Jinnah. When Liaquat Ali Khan and Begum Ra'ana Liaquat lived in London, they maintained a close association with Jinnah. Jinnah often played bridge with Begum Liaquat. It is said that they used to meet almost every evening, and Jinnah appreciated her wit and intellect. There were rumours that Jinnah's sister Fatima and Begum Ra'ana never got along with each other due to Jinnah's alleged fascination with the latter.

Liaquat Ali Khan faced many ups and downs during his tenure as prime minister of Pakistan. He had differences of opinion with Jinnah on the Kashmir issue: Liaquat Ali Khan wanted a diplomatic solution to resolve the problem and wanted to hold talks with Jawaharlal Nehru, whereas Jinnah wanted to capture Kashmir with the help of the army. It is believed that when all the prominent leaders were engaged in discussions about Partition, Sardar Patel had proposed to Liaquat Ali that he give up claim over Hyderabad and take Kashmir instead. However, the latter did not agree to it. There is no strong evidence supporting the existence of any such deal or claim though. Additionally, apart from being in a tussle with Fatima, Liaquat Ali was also at loggerheads with communist leaders in Pakistan.

After the demise of Jinnah, Liaquat Ali Khan succumbed to the hard-line Islamism practised by the top leaders of the newly formed Pakistan. The very foundation of Jinnah's Pakistan was shattered after his death, and every non-Muslim who became a part of Pakistan feared for his/her fundamental rights. Therefore, in order to safeguard their property, many Hindus and Sikhs living there decided to convert to Islam out of fear, though they never changed their surnames. That is why, even today, there are many Muslims with surnames like Sehgal, Kapur, Talwar, Malik, Rana, Bajwa and so on. The name of Pakistan's current army chief is also Qamar Javed Bajwa.

Liaquat Ali Khan was very special to Muhammad Ali Jinnah, and he was seen as his second-in-command. Jinnah had made him the first prime minister of Pakistan. Liaquat was intelligent and adept in political stratagems. Jahanara Shahnawaz, one of the most prominent leaders of the Muslim League, mentions that she was having dinner at Karachi's Palace Hotel on 13 August 1947, a day before Jinnah's swearing-in ceremony as governor-general of newly formed Pakistan. She was accompanied by the then premier of Bengal, Huseyn Shaheed Suhrawardy, Abul Hassan Isphani, a prominent leader of the All India Muslim League, and Altaf Hussain, the editor of *Dawn* (Karachi). Suddenly, news broke out that the new cabinet of ministers had been finalized. Someone by the name of Fazlur Rahman from Bengal was included in the cabinet whom even Suhrawardy and the leaders of the Bengal Muslim League did not know. Shaheed Suhrawardy and Hasan Isphani were so disappointed with the list of ministers who were included from East Pakistan that they got up from the dinner table and decided to leave.

All the capable and known Muslim League leaders were ignored. Leaders like Nawab Muhammad Ismail Khan and Raja

Sahab of Mahmoodabad, who were considered the foundation of the Muslim League, were treated as if they were dispensable. According to Jahanara Shahnawaz, this was Liaquat Ali Khan's doing. He had given the posts of ministers to all those he favoured, who were in fact incompetent at running the government, and all the good and capable leaders, especially the most important leaders of the working committee, were ignored. This is probably what led to the downfall of Pakistan soon after its formation. There was massive resentment amongst the Bengali Muslim League leaders regarding the attitude of Liaquat Ali Khan; so much so that they formed a new party called Awami League which stood against the Muslim League in East Pakistan.

Liaquat Ali Khan started promoting and endorsing only the people who were very close to him in almost every state, and no other leader, irrespective of how capable they may have been, was allowed to rise. In elections, tickets of the Muslim League were given to weak and incapable politicians, and this could have been the reason why the government of the Muslim League came to an end in the next ten years, followed by a coup d'état. General Ayub Khan formed the government at that time and marked the beginning of military rule in Pakistan because of which the whole nation suffered. Due to Ayub Khan's election fraud, even Fatima Jinnah lost the elections. However, some believe that the public was fed up with the Muslim League's rule and Jinnah's stature and had lost respect for them.

Ra'ana Liaquat Khan aka 'Almora ki Beti'

Now I would like to throw some light on Ra'ana Liaquat Khan, aka Sheila Pant, who played an important role in the movement for the creation of Pakistan and also afterwards. She was a well-respected and loved figure in undivided India. She was one of the leading and pioneering women in the Pakistan Movement and served as the executive member of the Pakistan Movement committee working under Muhammad Ali Jinnah. She was also known as 'Almora ki beti' (daughter of Almora) as she was born in Almora. As First Lady of Pakistan, she initiated reforms for women and child development and social progress and played a major role in paving the way for women to participate in Pakistan's politics.

In 1947, as the refugees began to pour in from across the border under the most pitiable of conditions, with cholera, diarrhoea and smallpox being common health issues plaguing them, Ra'ana called upon women to come forward and aid the situation by collecting food and medical supplies from various places to send them to the refugee camps. Ra'ana Liaquat formed a committee comprising several women who were helping her in this endeavour. These women were criticized by certain sections of society and also by some newspapers merely for stepping out of the four walls of their house. During this point in Pakistan's history, there were not many female nurses in Karachi, so Begum Liaquat asked the Army to train women to give injections and first aid. Women were then trained in three- to six-month courses and the paramilitary forces comprising women were formed. The Pakistan Army quickly established Army Medical Corps and recruited a high number of women nurses.

In 1949, Ra'ana arranged a conference of over 100 women from all over Pakistan. The conference announced the formation of a voluntary and non-political organization for the social, educational and cultural uplift of women; it was named All Pakistan Women's Association (APWA). She was nominated as its first president, and unlike the Pakistan Women National Group (PWNG), the APWA continued to grow as it remained active in working towards women's rights in Pakistan.

When Liaquat Ali Khan was assassinated in 1951, Ra'ana Liaquat was isolated for many years from Pakistan's politics. In 1972, after the creation of Bangladesh and after Pakistan went through an intense crisis, Ra'ana joined hands with the then president, Zulfikar Ali Bhutto, and became part of his government.

As minister of finance in Bhutto's government, she played an influential role in economic decisions. Bhutto encouraged her to participate in the upcoming elections, and Ra'ana won the elections in 1973. Bhutto did not waste time in appointing Ra'ana as the governor of Sindh province. She was the first female governor of that province and the first chancellor of Sindh University and Karachi University. She continued her term until 1976. Ra'ana again contested the 1977 parliamentary elections but did not take gubernatorial office due to martial law imposed by General Zia-ul-Haq, the chief of army staff of the Pakistan Army.

Later, she served as the ambassador of Pakistan to the Netherlands. But after that, she never really played an active role in politics. Ra'ana strongly opposed General Zia-ul-Haq after Bhutto was sentenced to death. Though General Zia was quite angry with her, he could not do much about it as she had a strong positive image amongst the people of Pakistan.

Though Ra'ana Liaquat tried to persuade her husband not to encourage Muslim fundamentalism, under the pressure of Jamaat-e-Islaam leaders, all the rights of the minorities were taken away and Liaquat Ali Khan did not do much about it. Ra'ana Liaquat was a lady of secular credentials and she also strongly opposed General Zia-ul-Haq's move to impose sharia in Pakistan.

Begum Ra'ana Liaquat died on 13 June 1990 and was buried next to her husband in the precincts of the Quaid-e-Azam's Mausoleum. With her, a historic period ended in Pakistan. The women and the youth of Pakistan continue to find inspiration from her life to work towards the emancipation of women and a more inclusive and progressive society.

Fatima Jinnah

Though Jinnah famously said that 'I alone with the help of my secretary and my typewriter won Pakistan', it is a known fact that Fatima played a crucial role in her brother's fight to create Pakistan. However, it appeared that the citizens of the country failed to honour her. Later, I believe, Fatima led a very lonely and unfulfilled life. When I travelled to Karachi, I paid a visit to her house, which was by then in a dilapidated condition. Surprisingly, it had not even been made into a memorial. Moreover, she seems to have died under mysterious circumstances. Fatima was living in her house with a cat and a servant. Her dead body was found in the house, and her servant—who had allegedly murdered her—was absconding. The reality is not known to anyone, and the government of the time tried its best to put a lid on the issue. Officially, it was maintained that she died due to a heart attack on 9 July 1967.

At the time, Pakistan was under military rule, and Ayub Khan had won the presidential elections by fraudulently defeating Fatima Jinnah. In the election, Fatima had support from leaders like Mujib-ur-Rahman from East Pakistan, the Pathan leader Khan Abdul Ghaffar Khan and Khan Abdul Wali Khan. Since Khan Abdul Gaffar Khan alias Seemant Gandhi was close to Mahatma Gandhi and Nehru, his support to Fatima led to Ayub Khan portraying her as India's stooge in the election. Ayub Khan had launched a campaign against her propagating that India and America wanted to put Fatima on Pakistan's throne as their candidate. This cost Fatima dearly and she lost the elections.

Ayub Khan stooped to new lows during these elections and put the entire country to shame. In Gujranwala, he once paraded a female dog with a lantern around its neck. It was certainly an attack on Fatima as the lantern was her election symbol. Following her defeat in these elections, she began to excuse herself from public and stayed away from the public eye till she passed away in 1967. After her mysterious death, a leader named Ghulam Sarwar Malik demanded an investigation to ascertain the cause of her death and filed a petition that was accepted in a regional court of the country in 1972. He claimed that there were wounds on her body and wanted her corpse to be exhumed and sent for forensic investigation; but the then government turned a deaf ear to his pleas. Fatima's nephew, Akbar Peer Bhai, had also demanded a forensic investigation, but the government simply ignored it. Just a day before her death, Fatima was said to have gone to attend a wedding and was seemingly fit and happy. It is alleged* that President Ayub Khan was responsible for her death since she was a threat to his political career. Also, the Muslim fundamentalists never considered her to be a 'true' Muslim since she was Khoja Ismaili Muslim, a fact that they could not stand.

Fatima had a degree in dentistry from Calcutta and practised in her own clinic. She was known to be a short-tempered woman. Despite the fact that Jinnah was amongst the prominent leaders who always promoted unity between Hindus and Muslims and was also married to a non-Muslim, Fatima played an important role in making him follow Islam strictly. After the formation of Pakistan, Fatima became the kingmaker and held sway over other Muslim League leaders. She also did not get along with Ra'ana Liaquat and didn't allow her to meet Jinnah much. Her ideology with regard to Pakistan was apparent when she recorded a radio broadcast on the third death anniversary of her brother and Pakistan's Quaid-e-Azam, in which she recorded her thoughts on the situation in Pakistan and how it was different from what her elder brother Jinnah had envisioned. Parts of her message, where she criticized the government, were left out of the broadcast, citing technical glitches. Radio Pakistan had earlier requested her to omit those lines, a request that Fatima had denied. Following the incident, she angrily wrote a letter to the Radio Pakistan head, Zulfiqar Ali Bukhari, where she criticized the censoring of freedom of speech by a democratic government.

---

* See http://content.time.com/time/subscriber/article/0,33009,830952,00.html.

Even earlier she had gotten into a dispute with the first president of the democratically elected government of Pakistan, Iskander Ali Mirza, who initiated the process of enforcing martial law on Pakistan by appointing Ayub Khan as his deputy from the Pakistan Army. In a span of a few days, Mirza's relation with Ayub Khan became conflicted as he replaced Mirza and became the martial law administrator of Pakistan himself and later became the president. This move was welcomed by Fatima initially, but later, she realized that Ayub Khan's intentions were worse than those of Iskandar Mirza, and subsequently she was at loggerheads with Ayub Khan as well.

Fatima Jinnah was buried at Mazar-e-Quaid (Jinnah's final resting place) and so was Liaquat Ali Khan. Both of them were buried near the tomb of Muhammad Ali Jinnah.

It was on 16 October 1951 that Liaquat Ali Khan was shot dead while addressing a public meeting in the Company Bagh at Rawalpindi. It was speculated that Khan's death would pave the way to a united Pashtunistan. Benazir Bhutto, another famous politician, was also assassinated in 2007 in the same manner at the same place, which had been renamed Liaquat National Bagh. The reason why both of them were killed and who were behind their assassinations remain mysteries till today.

10

The Lost Royalty

Abida Sultan and Her Whip

The family of the Nawab of Bhopal, a very wealthy princely state in British India and the current capital of Madhya Pradesh in India, is another family that did not get due credit for its contribution to Pakistan. For this, we must go into the history of the Bhopal royal family.

The Nawab of Bhopal, Hajji Nawab Hafiz Sir Hamidullah Khan, had no son. He had three daughters named Abida, Sajida and Rabia. He himself had taken over the reigns of the royal court from his mother, Sarkar Amma—Bhopal was at the time ruled by a matriarch. Sarkar Amma, aka Sultan Jahan, fought with the British to allow her favourite son to become the king of the state. After the Nawab, Abida Sultan, his eldest daughter, was declared the heir apparent to be crowned the queen of Bhopal. Abida Sultan was of strong physical built and a very active woman who rode horses, played golf and even drove a jeep. The Nawab got Abida married to Muhammad Sarwar Ali Khan, the nawab of the small princely state of Kurwai. They were blessed with a son, who was named Shahryar Khan. However, Abida did not get along with Sarwar Ali and within a year of their marriage, they separated. As per the rules of the Bhopal state then, it was the father who became the legal guardian of the son in case of a separation and not the mother. As narrated by Mr Sharyar Khan, son of Abida Sultan, it is believed that Abida Sultan could not digest this and drove in her jeep to the palace of Kurwai, hit her husband with a *chabuk* (whip) when he resisted parting with their son and brought her son to Bhopal.

Abida lived her own life in Bhopal. She was an outstanding sportsperson and played polo, bicycle polo, hockey, cricket and squash, among many other sports that were traditionally dominated by men. Her tough and headstrong character was shaped by her grandmother Sikander Begum. Just before the Second World War, Abida took on the onus of running the state on behalf of her father who became a more prominent figure in the contemporary political scenario—the imminent point of the division of the country. Abida was a fearless crack shot with guns and had killed seventy-two tigers in her time. She was the second Muslim woman in South Asia to be given a pilot's licence. She participated in the All-India Women's Squash Championship in the year 1948, where she bagged the top spot in her maiden entry.

By the time Shahryar, her son, turned four, she adopted two more boys, Sultan Mal from a Hindu family and Syed Farooq Ali from a Muslim family, to aid the spiritual and intellectual growth of her only son. In the morning, they would take lessons together in Urdu and learn the Quran and the teachings of Islam with a Wahhabi scholar, followed by lessons in English, mathematics, geography, history, science, calligraphy and the arts with an English governess. The afternoons and evenings were reserved for sports, learning crafts and musical instruments. Later, she sent her son to the Royal Indian Military College in Dehradun as well so that he could learn discipline and understand diverse cultures by living with peers from different religious backgrounds.

Another fascinating incident relating to Abida Sultan that is often narrated by Shahryar is from the day when Gandhi was assassinated. He narrates,

On 30 January 1948, we were at school [Daly College], playing cricket and hockey, and suddenly the news came that Mahatma Gandhi had been assassinated. This was a huge shock. Everyone was stunned, even people like us who were carefree. Before that, there were no tensions between Hindus and Muslims. There were only twelve to thirteen Muslim boys in college. They hadn't announced the name of the assassin for six hours. During those six hours, there was always a possibility that a Muslim might have done it. If that had happened, then all hell would have broken loose against Muslims. My mother got into a station wagon and drove a straight hundred miles to Indore to the college. She told the principal B.G. Miller that she was going to take all the Muslim boys, and the principal said he couldn't let them go without their parents' permission. To this she replied that if something happened to them, then he would be responsible for not letting them come with her back to the safety of Bhopal. He eventually allowed her to take us all. We were all packed into the station wagon like sardines and taken to Bhopal. We drove for four hours and by then it was known that a right-wing Hindu had assassinated Gandhi. In a sense we were relieved, but it was a very bad time for us.[*]

It is said that the effect of this incident sowed the seeds of worry in the mind of Abida Sultan about the future of her son, a Muslim prince, in India.

---

[*] S. Khan, *Oral History with Shaharyar Khan*, 31 May 2016. https://exhibits.stanford.edu/. Retrieved from https://exhibits.stanford.edu/1947-partition/catalog/gh485jy8250.

Abida Sultan had a major fallout with her father, Hamidullah Khan, Nawab of Bhopal, over his second marriage, in spite of her being her father's greatest support, confidante and favourite child. She was ordered to pay reverence to a new begum after her mother had been a dedicated consort of her father for forty-five years. Abida Sultan's father married Aftab Jahan Begum Sahiba in 1947 and Abida Sultan's mother was sidelined, which she could never come to terms with. In the year 1949, without informing anyone, she took a train to Bombay and the next day boarded a ship to London, from where she planned to migrate to Pakistan. She carried only her personal jewellery and left behind an entire fortune that consisted of palaces, servants, *jagirs* (vast tracts of lands), *shikargahs* (rest homes in jungles for hunting), an arsenal of rifles and invaluable artefacts. She sold her jewellery and used the proceeds from the sale to finance her emigration to Pakistan and her son Shahryar's education at the University of Cambridge. Her father withdrew all financial support. For a long time, she lived without any electricity in a small house in Malir on the outskirts of Karachi that she built for herself. The stand-off with her father went on till the end of the Nawab's life.

When I spoke to her son Shahryar Khan, who is a good friend of mine, he told me that the then high commissioner of India in London, Krishna Menon, tried to convince his mother to return to India instead of settling in Pakistan. He told her that in India, she would be the queen of Bhopal with wealth that was worth billions. He told her that in the future, she could live as a renowned figure in independent India. Though Krishna Menon was her friend, she turned a deaf ear to him and, in 1950, travelled to Karachi from London and became a citizen of Pakistan.

In one of her interviews, she spoke about her conversation with Jinnah immediately after Partition. Jinnah envisioned her as Pakistan's voice in the United Nations (UN). He wanted her to be Pakistan's representative the same way that the Indian Prime Minister Jawaharlal Nehru's sister, Vijaya Laxmi Pandit, was

India's. But that could never happen as Jinnah passed away before she settled down in Pakistan. In the same interview, she claimed that after the death of Jinnah, her father was supposed to become the governor-general of Pakistan, but that too never happened.

After she went to Pakistan, the government did not give Abida any importance and the subsequent governments that came into power along with the then president Ayub Khan never gave her the status that she could have enjoyed in India as Nawab Gowhar-i-Taj, Abida Sultan Begum Sahiba of Bhopal. The only prestige that was granted to her by the government of Pakistan was when she was sent to Brazil as an ambassador for a very brief period.

The Nawab of Bhopal had properties worth billions. Not only that, he had a huge property in Saudi Arabia in Mecca, which was near Kaaba. It is a well-known fact that during the time, the government of Saudi Arabia was not very rich and expenses to maintain Mecca were given by the nawabs of India, in lieu of which they were given lands there to build *rabats* (guest houses for Muslim pilgrims).

The moment she became a citizen of Pakistan, she lost the right to claim the Bhopal throne, and after the demise of the Nawab of Bhopal in 1960, his younger daughter Sajida Sultan became the legal heir and queen of Bhopal. She was married to Nawab Iftikhar Ali Khan of the princely state of Pataudi situated near Delhi. He was a cricketer. Mansoor Ali Khan 'Tiger' Pataudi was their son, also a famous cricketer, who married the famous actress Sharmila Tagore and was later blessed with three children, two of whom are well-known film stars, Saif Ali Khan and Soha Ali Khan. The third sibling, Saba Ali Khan, is a famous jewellery designer and chief trustee of Auqf-e-Shahi (Royal Trust) established by the princely state of Bhopal as a royal charitable endowment to manage the rabats in Bhopal. The trust got millions of rupees in compensation from the Saudi government a few years ago when its rabats in Saudi Arabia were taken over by the government for the expansion of the Kaaba in Mecca. Kareena Kapoor is the daughter-in-law of the Nawab of Pataudi as she is married to Saif Ali Khan.

Nawab Hamidullah owned a property by the name of Bhopal House in Karachi, half of which was overtaken by the Pakistan government for office use; the other half still belongs to Shahryar. Instead of honouring the great Abida Sultan who sacrificed her royal fortune and title to move to Pakistan, the government of Pakistan did not even let them keep what was rightfully theirs, especially at a time when many other people were being allotted properties.

The ownership of the rest of the properties in Bhopal was transferred to Tiger Pataudi's family as his mother Sajida Sultan was the queen of Bhopal, Abida Sultan having abdicated the throne. Abida and her son Shahryar Khan could not legally claim anything in India since they were now citizens of Pakistan. However, according to British law, the properties in Bhopal could be distributed equally among all the daughters, whether they were living in India or Pakistan. In Pakistan, according to the sharia law, the properties of Nawab Hamidullah Khan could be equally distributed among all the heirs.

Abida was the legal heir of not only Nawab Hamidullah and Bhopal's legacy, but her former husband, Nawab Kurwai's as well. According to sources close to her, before her death, Abida wrote a letter to her son Shahryar Khan in which she regretted her decision of leaving Bhopal and letting go of a great inheritance and fortune that would have passed on to Shahryar had she stayed in India.

Shahryar Khan entered the foreign services of Pakistan on his own merit and, in 1990, became the foreign secretary of the country. He was well respected in the field of diplomacy and was considered one of the best diplomats. Apart from that, he is still a well-known figure in the country, having served as the chairman of the Pakistan Cricket Board twice. He married Minal aka, Minnoo, who was the daughter of the former foreign secretary and Pakistan Ambassador Syed Akhtar Hussain, who hailed from Bareilly, Uttar Pradesh, and was an Indian Civil Services officer in undivided India. He had close ties with Nehru and even named his elder daughter Indira after Nehru's daughter. But after Partition, he opted to move to Pakistan and joined the Pakistan Foreign Services and became a very well-known diplomat.

Even today, Shahryar Khan has great respect for India and played a vital role in the historic Indo-Pakistan cricket series held in 2004. Both Shahryar Khan and his wife Minnoo are quite popular in India and have many friends in the country. I often joked with Shahryar that he became a foreign secretary in Pakistan, but had his mother decided to stay back in India he would have become the foreign minister in this country! Rajiv Gandhi gave an election ticket to Shahryar's cousin 'Tiger' Pataudi in 1991, and he contested from his home turf in Bhopal; but he lost the election and did not dabble in politics any further.

Shahryar Khan and Minnoo shared family relations with well-known politician and former finance minister of India, the late Arun Jaitley, as well. Shahryar also served as the high commissioner of Pakistan in London; nowadays he resides in Lahore. He was born in 1934 and is still physically very active. Pervez Musharraf appointed him as the chairman of the Pakistan Cricket Board in 2003 and he again served as its chairman in August 2014; above all, he also became the head of the Asia Cricket Council. Even in his advanced age, he teaches at the Lahore University of Management Sciences as a professor of foreign policy.

Cricket and Royalty

It is a very interesting fact that Shahryar's uncle, Iftikhar Ali Khan Pataudi (Sajida Begum's husband) and his son (also Shahryar's first cousin), Tiger Pataudi, both had the honour of serving as captains of the Indian cricket team. There is an intriguing story behind the captaincy of Iftikhar Ali Khan.

There was a cricketer by the name of Bhausaheb Babasaheb Nimbalkar who used to play for Maharashtra. He is the only cricketer to have got to a quadruple hundred in a domestic tournament by scoring an unbeaten 443 runs in the 1948–49 season. This is also the highest score for any cricketer who has not played test cricket. At the time, he was second only to Sir Don Bradman who scored 452 runs and, currently, it is the fourth-highest score of all-time. Nimbalkar's team were at 826/4 at lunch break and he was all set to break the record of Don. But, the opposition captain, Thakore Saheb of Rajkot, conceded the match by running away in the night before the last day of play without informing anyone in order to prevent the team from any more embarrassment. Sir Don Bradman later wrote a letter to Bhausaheb Nimbalkar saying that Nimbalkar's innings were better than his own.

Looking at this great inning, it was decided that B.B. Nimbalkar would be made the captain of the Indian cricket team for an upcoming England cricket tour. In those days, cricket players at the top were mostly from the royal families due to their proximity to the British and hence their exposure to the game. Nimbalkar was from an ordinary family and none of the players could digest the fact that they would have to play under the captainship of a 'commoner'. Hence, it was decided that Iftikhar Ali Pataudi would be made the captain of the team and not Nimbalkar since Iftikhar was a Nawab.

Allama Muhammad Iqbal

There was another well-known family that played an important role in the creation of Pakistan whom Pakistan failed to honour. Allama Muhammad Iqbal was a great poet in British India who composed the famous patriotic song *Saare jaahan se accha, Hindostaan humara.* Iqbal was originally a Kashmiri Pandit and Tej Bahadur Sapru—a prominent Indian freedom fighter, lawyer, politician and key figure who helped in drafting the Indian Constitution—was his first cousin. He was also an advocate of Hindu–Muslim unity. *Mazhab nahi sikhata aapas mein bair rakhna,*

Hindu hain hum, watan hai Hindustan humara is from the song written by him. Later, however, he also supported the proposal of a separate nation.

Allama Iqbal graduated from Cambridge in 1905 and studied law in England thereafter. Later, he completed his PhD from Germany and returned to Lahore. When he passed away in 1938, a grand tomb was built inside the Lahore Fort where he was buried—such was the extent of his respect in the country. He had a son named Javed Iqbal and a daughter named Munira Baano from his third wife, Sardar Begum. They both were quite capable and highly educated, but the government in Pakistan did not give them their due.

Not only that, the son-in-law of Iqbal was Mian Iftikharuddin, who was the chairman of the United Punjab Congress Committee till Partition and was a good friend of Nehru. Iftikharuddin used to stay at the Government Officers Residence in Lahore, and Indira Gandhi would also stay over at his house every time she travelled to Lahore from Allahabad before Partition. Despite being Allama Iqbal's son-in-law and a politician, he was not given any importance in the newly formed Pakistan. Iftikharuddin joined the Muslim League, but other leaders of the party did not give him a chance to progress in his career.

Mian Iftikharuddin's son Yousuf Salahuddin, also known as Yousuf Salli, still lives in Lahore. He has many Indians friends, including me. He has been doing a lot to promote Indo-Pak friendship for the last few decades through cultural activities. Yousuf became a musician and for the past thirty years, has been encouraging the singers and the musicians of India and Pakistan. He has played a vital role in bringing together artists from both countries and taking forward their friendship. To welcome the Indian cricket team in Lahore, he hosted a party at his mansion. This mansion boasts of sixteenth-century Mughal era architecture and is situated in the Barood Khana area in front of the Lahore Fort. Yousuf loves to throw parties and invite the glitterati from different countries. His parties often become the talk of the town, with guests comprising A-listers from the Pakistani and Indian elite. He has inherited his cultural inclination from his grandfather, which clearly reflects in his lifestyle and initiatives. It is Yousuf who is credited with bringing back to life the famous Basant festival of Lahore.

I am proud to have Yousuf Salli as a good friend. He once showed me all the letters that Nehru and Indira Gandhi wrote to his parents. In 1983, he had come to Delhi to meet Indira Gandhi with all her letters, and the fondness was reciprocated by Indira Gandhi as the moment she came to know about his arrival, she invited him over for a meal to the prime minister's residence.

11

The Inevitable Separation
The 1971 Bangladesh War

Regional Biases

Jinnah's Pakistan lacked the idea of unity from the very beginning. After Partition a separate Muslim country did come into existence, but the population divided themselves into Punjabis, Sindhis, Balochs, Pathans and Muhajirs. The Punjabis formed up to 60 per cent of the total population of Pakistan and adopted Punjabi as their preferred language. Punjabiyat* is so deeply rooted in this section of the population that its attitude towards non-Punjabis proved to be downright condescending and antagonistic. Muhajirs are the Muslims who migrated to Pakistan from states other than Punjab (India) such as Uttar Pradesh (UP), Madhya Pradesh and Bihar. They were treated very unfairly. I once visited Pakistan to conduct an interview for my TV programme *Ru-Ba-Ru*. The local Pakistani cameraman named Mehboob, who originally hailed from

---

* See https://www.dailypioneer.com/2013/book-reviews/in-search-of-the-punjabiyat.html.

the Nizamuddin area of Delhi, told me that till his last breath his father maintained that the biggest mistake of his life was coming to Pakistan. Mehboob's father hailed from Meerut (UP) and later started living in the Nizamuddin locality of Delhi. He shifted to Karachi in 1947. Mehboob claimed his father often said that had he decided to live in India, he would have enjoyed his life. However, in Pakistan, he used to feel as if there was a raging ocean in front of him while the rifles of the Punjabis and the Sindhis were pointing at his back. He never felt he had a chance to live peacefully in Pakistan. He said that most of the Muhajir families had lost someone to bullets fired by Punjabis or Sindhis.

I was once in Islamabad, where I was staying in a hotel, for the South Asian Association for Regional Cooperation (SAARC) conference. Kuldeep Nayar and Rajendra Sarin, the famous Indian journalist of Pakistani affairs, were also staying there. Many influential Pakistani politicians and officers used to come over to meet them at the hotel every evening. All of them used to converse with Nayar and Sarin in Punjabi and treat them like brothers. But whenever an Indian Muslim journalist attended the evening meeting, they would all quietly ask Nayar and Sarin to ask those journalists to leave as they did not feel comfortable around the Muhajirs. I was very young at that time and all these renowned people somehow thought that I was Punjabi too. I would sit amongst them and enjoyed listening to their conversations and tales of Punjabi unity.

While returning to India from the conference, I was with Rajiv Gandhi in his aircraft, and he told me that Benazir Bhutto and he had become good friends and she had promised him that she would work towards improving relations between India and Pakistan; but she also said that the interference of the army was so over-reaching that despite her being the prime minister of Pakistan, no decision could be implemented without the army's consent. The army chief had to be taken into consideration in every matter.

I still remember those words of Rajiv Gandhi; it is completely true that no matter how many governments are democratically elected in Pakistan, they have to work under the army chief. Every elected prime minister in Pakistan feared the army might resort to subversion of the government. Nawaz Sharif and Zulfikar Ali Bhutto experienced it. General Zia-ul-Haq sentenced Zulfikar Ali Bhutto to death even after severe opposition from the people of Pakistan. General Zia was also a Punjabi from Jalandhar and had completed his studies from St Stephen's College, Delhi. His family was quite friendly with Indian film actor Shatrughan Sinha. When I visited Islamabad, I went to General Zia's house in Rawalpindi. Though Zia was no more, his son Ijaz-ul-Haq was there. He is well-educated and a person of serious disposition. I spoke to him for hours. He worked as a banker in a high post; he also tried his best to succeed in politics, but unfortunately he could not. When Zia-ul-Haq was serving as the president, he preferred to reside in the army chief's house in Rawalpindi instead of the President's House in Islamabad. He was once travelling to Islamabad from Bahawalpur in an aircraft. As it turned out, someone had planted a bomb in the aircraft and Zia died in the blast.

Moving on, the people from the Punjab region of Pakistan always felt that had India not been partitioned, Punjabis would have dominated from Peshawar (situated near the North-West Frontier Province in Pakistan) to Palwal (a city in present-day Haryana in India), and there would have been around 250 members from their clan in the Indian Parliament and every prime minister would have been from the Punjab region because of the sheer prominence of the community.

The regional prejudice of Punjabis and Sindhis exists across Pakistan to such an extent that even the most capable and deserving Mujahirs are not allowed to serve in high posts in the government. Similarly, the Punjabis and the Sindhis also fought with each other, and neither got along with the Balochs.

Jinnah and a Case for Pakistan

The Balochs considered themselves entirely different from the others. The founding father of Pakistan, Muhammad Ali Jinnah, used to give a lot of importance to Baluchistan. His last journey was to Quetta, where he had gone to express his affinity with the Balochs. There he fell sick and was brought back to Karachi in an air force plane. The ambulance in which Jinnah was being taken to his downtown residence from the Karachi airbase broke down on the way. The ambulance had no backup and Jinnah had to wait for two hours on a stretcher for a replacement ambulance in the oppressive, humid autumn heat of the city by the Arabian Sea. He passed away later that evening.

Jinnah had a medical history of tuberculosis. His doctor was a Parsi Patel who knew well in advance that he would not survive for more than six months, but he never divulged that information to Gandhi and Nehru at the behest of Jinnah's sister, Fatima. Historians believe that had Gandhi, Nehru and Sardar Patel been aware of this fact, the partition of the nation might have been avoided and millions of lives could have been saved.

Moreover, Mahatma Gandhi had a clear argument against Partition—all the Muslims of India, he believed, were primarily Hindus who became Muslim later. How could there be a nation of converts? A separate country for converts was not a good idea. They were all our brothers. Their attitude, appearance, eating habits, etc., were all the same. Then where was the need to create a separate country for them and distance them from ourselves? When the Cabinet Mission came to India, Jinnah countered Gandhi's argument by saying that that during the era of Chandragupta Maurya, Indians were not alike; there was a mix of people with completely different backgrounds and cultures. He also argued that Hindus and Muslims have completely different habits and cultures. According to him, the figure of 70 per cent Muslim population being converts was correct, but that happened because many converted to Islam from Hinduism since they were being tortured by the Hindu community.

Jinnah had posed many other unsubstantiated arguments as well. For example, according to M.J. Akbar's book, Jinnah is known to have claimed that whenever a Hindu shook his hands with a Muslim, he washed his hands thinking they had been dirtied, but the Cabinet Mission did not seem to be in agreement with that. One of the members of the Cabinet Mission, Stafford, argued with Jinnah saying that if what he was saying was true, then the Pathan Muslims were also totally different from Bengali Muslims. They had a different appearance, language, dressing style and culture as well. So why should there be a single country for them? Jinnah had no answer to his questions and skirted the issue. The then viceroy, Archibald Wavell, was also not at all convinced of Jinnah's arguments.

Maulana Azad met the leaders of the Mission and strongly opposed the arguments and points raised by Jinnah. He further added that the formation of a separate nation for the Muslims was a step against their fundamental rights. Maulana Azad referred to Hazrat Muhammad, who was also against any kind of partition or division between people. For him, the whole world was one nation, the whole world was one big mosque. In the end, Gandhi advised Wavell to make Jinnah the leader of the first national government of India, where, naturally, both Hindus and Muslims would serve as ministers, and if he was able to run the government successfully, it would become clear that there was no need for a separate country. But unfortunately, Jinnah did not agree with Gandhi on that front either. This episode has been explained in detail by renowned journalist M.J. Akbar in his book *Gandhi's Hinduism: The Struggle against Jinnah's Islam.* Another Pakistani historian, Istihaaq Hussain Qureshi, supported Jinnah's argument that the Muslims of India were converts from Hinduism in his book *The Struggle for Pakistan.* He mentioned that in the past, many Muslims from Arab countries, along with other Muslim nations, came to India and started living here. Qureshi has also claimed that whenever a Muslim visited any Hindu's house, they were served food in separate utensils.

Ultimately, Jinnah was successful in pressuring the British to form a separate nation, Pakistan, with his arguments. Jinnah had made a deal with Viceroy Linlithgow at the time of the onset of the Second World War. During the war, Britain needed all the help that it could get from India, which was its best source for men and material. Without support from India, Adolf Hitler's defeat of Britain and its allies was inevitable. The terms for the deal were simple; Jinnah would offer Muslim support to the British war effort and in return Viceroy Linlithgow would give him an undertaking that there would be no settlement on the future structure of India without Muslim concurrence. Here, the Muslims were represented by the Muslim League and the Muslim League was Jinnah himself. Out of a total of 4,18,000 Indian men who were deployed in the British Army during the first year of the war, 1,55,000 or 37 per cent men were Muslims. Nearly half of the total army or 2,01,000 men came from the Punjab region, which back then stretched from the edge of Delhi to the Hindu Kush, and about half of these recruits were Muslims.

It is interesting to note that a large number of Hindu families are purely vegetarian; it is possible they might have used separate utensils for Muslims, but that could be due to the fact that Muslims eat non-vegetarian food and not because of them being Muslim. Nowadays, I have not seen or heard about any incident where a Hindu feels the need to wash his hands every time he shakes his hand with a Muslim. But at the time of Independence, Jinnah's arguments unfortunately became quite appealing, and on the advice of Gandhi, Rajagopalachari and Maulana Azad met Viceroy Archibald Wavell to convince him against the Partition. Finally, the Cabinet Mission decided that instead of a separate nation, Punjab, Assam and Bengal would be divided; the new states would serve as autonomous Muslim states and would be subordinate to the national government, which would exercise its right to regulate their foreign, defence, finance and other affairs. The decision was also finalized in the sessions of the working committee of the All India Congress Committee (AICC). Jinnah agreed to the decision, but a large section of the Muslim League expressed a sense of dissatisfaction and hatred towards Jinnah due to this. They felt that if only state governments had to be brought into existence instead of a separate country, then where was the need to raise the urgent demand for a separate nation for so many years because of which so many Muslims had already lost their lives?

Consequently, Jinnah turned back on his decision and refused to accept the earlier proposal. Not only that, he also called for 'direct action' and formed a military force of young Muslims called the Muslim National Guard, which led to many riots. Many lives were lost during this time, and the situation deteriorated to such an extent that Nehru and Patel finally concluded that it was better to divide the nation instead of becoming witnesses to such mayhem.

The members of the Muslim League and Jinnah began to feel that the Congress as a party was earmarked for Hindus, and they claimed that Nehru and Gandhi were interested in protecting only the interests of Hindus. They felt a country ruled by the Congress with Jawaharlal Nehru as the leader of the government would only care for Hindus, and Muslims would always suffer and face injustice. Gandhi and Nehru tried their best to explain the consequences of these actions to Jinnah, Liaquat Ali Khan, Sardar Abdur Rab Nishtar (from Bengal) and other prominent leaders of the Muslim League, but they turned a deaf ear. On 2 June 1947, at the Viceroy House, when Mountbatten was about to put his final stamp on the plan to create a separate nation in the name of Pakistan, on one side of Mountbatten sat Jawaharlal Nehru, Sardar Patel, Acharya Kriplani and Sardar Baldev Singh, and on his other side, representing the Muslim League, were Muhammad Ali Jinnah, Liaquat Ali and Sardar Rao Nishtar. The Viceroy House is the Rashtrapati Bhawan of today. When Pranab Mukherjee became the president of India, he deeply studied these historical events in a sequential manner. He preserved all the furniture in the erstwhile Viceroy House and the room where the president meets people today still has the same table on which Lord Mountbatten finalized the division of the country. Pranab Mukherjee used to invite people to the Rashtrapati Bhawan to show this piece of furniture that had been witness to great historical events.

Finding Common Ground

In 1947, a new country named Pakistan came into existence, which became home to a people with the same culture, lifestyle, food habits, religion and belief system, without any diversity. Today, I believe, Jinnah's ideology that stood against the principle of unity in diversity seems to have failed. Why is India progressing today? It is because it has always been a country that welcomed people from different religious backgrounds, be it Hindus, Muslims, Sikhs, Parsis, Christians or Buddhists. All of them have immensely contributed to the development of the nation in various fields like politics, administration, arts, literature, music, films, commerce, etc. In fact, today, you may find people of Pakistan addressing their great artists by calling them the Amitabh Bachchan or Shah Rukh Khan of Pakistan.

In Pakistan's political landscape, there were many leaders who tried to extend a hand of friendship to India in spite of being under the pressure of military rule. One such person was my dear friend, Chaudhry Shujaat Hussain. He served as the prime minister of Pakistan for a very short duration, but his younger brother was the chief minister of Punjab, the largest state of Pakistan, for a long time. Hussain tried to improve trade relations with India during his tenure and on the request of Lal Krishna Advani, he got the Hindu temples of Katas Raj in Pakistan renovated. Katas Raj is a place that falls between Rawalpindi and Lahore, and many temples there had been shut for a long time and were turning into ruins. Hussain not only got these temples renovated but also, under his leadership, people started worshipping in these temples again.

He also tried to implement an idea with regard to sugarcane molasses grown in Pakistan, which is wasted due to the lack of permission to open liquor factories in the country as per the Islamic law. India, on the other hand, has many liquor factories. Hussain's idea was to sell Pakistani molasses to India at cheap prices. He got in touch with the then railway minister of India, Lalu Prasad Yadav, who was a friend of his, and requested for railway containers to transport molasses from Pakistan to India. Lalu Prasad also agreed to the proposal since it was a mutually beneficial deal, but due to some security concerns, the Union Ministry of Home Affairs intervened and did not give its consent to this decision.

Chaudhary Shujaat Hussain often entertained guests from India at his residence on Zahoor Elahi Road, Lahore. I once stayed over at his house when I was in the city. One day, I suddenly woke up at 6 a.m. when I heard some noises coming from the bathroom. To my surprise, Prime Minister Shujaat was arranging for toiletries for me and, at the same time, his brother, Chief Minister Chaudhary Parvez Elahi, was stocking up the fridge with juice and other beverages. I was overwhelmed with the hospitality I was extended. Hussain was so attached to India that he used to visit an Ayurvedic dispensary in Kerala for the treatment of his Parkinson's disease.

Prime Minister Nawaz Sharif also showed his willingness to maintain cordial and friendly relations with India. Vajpayee and Nawaz Sharif got along very well, because of which Vajpayee's bus journey to Lahore was quite successful. I have met Nawaz Sharif many times in Pakistan and London. He used to often visit an Indian restaurant in London, La Porte des Indes, situated at Marble Arch, to savour Indian food, and many a times we would bump into each other over there. He always supported the friendship between India and Pakistan. I had interviewed him in 1998 when he was serving as prime minister and he suggested that all those industries for which the raw materials are available in Pakistan should be set up in India and the ones which have their raw materials available in India should be established in Pakistan. In this manner, the industrialists on both sides of the border would be able to put pressure upon their governments to maintain peaceful relations between the countries. Sharif said that Pakistan purchased the cars of Suzuki made in Japan that cost around Rs 5 lakh and the same car by Maruti Suzuki could be purchased from India at a price of Rs 1.5 lakh without the extra cost of shipping. They could be easily brought to Pakistan via the Wagah border. Similarly, Pakistan purchased expensive motorcycles from Japan that could be purchased from Hero Honda in India at a much lower price. Nawaz Sharif had good relations with many industrialists in India, and his younger brother, Shahbaaz Sharif, who was once chief minister of Punjab in Pakistan, still has many friends amongst Indian industrialists and businessmen.

I also met Benazir Bhutto twice. She did not seem to have much interest in India and, moreover, her knowledge about India and its history seemed limited. She was very articulate and tactful in her interactions though. She always used to praise her husband no matter what anyone said about him.

One thing is absolutely clear: though Jinnah succeeded in creating Pakistan, the biggest controversy in the country was regarding the issue of West Pakistan and East Pakistan. The people of East Pakistan were mainly Bengali Muslims and were very poor. The Punjabis, Sindhis and Pathans of West Pakistan used to treat them with disdain and never accepted them as their fellow citizens. I believe it was because of this reason that Muhammad Ali Jinnah himself did not like Bengali Muslims; there was a wave of sadness all across East Pakistan as a result. Suhrawardy and the other prominent Bengali Muslim leaders were already upset with the kind of stepmotherly treatment being imparted to East

Pakistan, which was reflected during the creation of the cabinet as well. It was the result of this behaviour that on 23 June 1949, Suhrawardy and Abdul Hamid Khan Bhashani created the All Pakistan Awami League, which was a party of East Pakistan opposed to the Muslim League. Later, the movement culminated in the creation of a separate nation by Suhrawardy's main disciple Sheikh Mujib-ur-Rahman in 1971.

The demand for a separate country by East Pakistan resulted in a war between India and Pakistan in 1971, and ultimately Pakistan lost to India during Indira Gandhi's rule. A new country named Bangladesh came into existence thereafter. Had Jinnah and other leaders like Liaquat Ali Khan not turned their backs on the people of East Pakistan—which was followed by the torture meted out by Ayub Khan and Yahya Khan to the Bengali Muslims—Bangladesh would probably never have been created. At this point, I am reminded of the words of Lord Mountbatten's daughter, Pamela Hicks. She had written in her book *Daughter of Empire: My Life as a Mountbatten* that her mother always used to say that Pakistan's division was unrealistic. West Pakistan was on one end and East Pakistan on the other end, thousands of miles away, and in the middle, there was the huge country of India, at loggerheads with Pakistan. Her mother compared this partition to an elephant. There was a huge head of the elephant in the middle and two ears hanging on either sides. Pamela was absolutely correct; this partition was a not a good step. The people of West Pakistan had to take a very long and tortuous route to reach East Pakistan, and there was no synergy between them.

Later, when Sheikh Mujib, as the head of the All Pakistan Awami Muslim League, won the elections with a majority, instead of making him the prime minister, Yahya Khan charged him with treason. Due to this act by the authorities in West Pakistan, civil disobedience erupted across East Pakistan, and Mujib indirectly announced the independence of East Pakistan from West Pakistan during a landmark speech on 7 March 1971. On 26 March 1971, the Pakistan Army responded to the mass protests with Operation Searchlight, in which the prime minister-elect Mujib was arrested and flown to solitary confinement in West Pakistan, while Bengali civilians, students, intellectuals, politicians and military defectors were murdered as part of the 1971 Bangladesh genocide. Prime Minister Indira Gandhi on 27 March 1971 expressed the full support of her government for the independence struggle of the people of East Pakistan.

Between April 1971 and November 1971, Indira Gandhi garnered international support for the cause of East Pakistan and highlighted the atrocities committed by West Pakistani authorities and its army. The most important support came from the Soviet Union, which expressed its sympathies with East Pakistanis and supported Mukti Bahini's incursion* against West Pakistan during the war. The Soviet Union gave assurance to India that if a confrontation with the United States or China occurred, it would take countermeasures. This assurance was enshrined in the Indo-Soviet Treaty of Friendship and Cooperation signed in August 1971.

During Mujib's absence, many Bengalis joined the Mukti Bahini and defeated the Pakistani Armed Forces during the Bangladesh Liberation War. After Bangladesh's independence, Mujib was released from Pakistani custody due to international pressure and returned to Dhaka in January 1972 after a short visit to Britain and India.

Sheikh Mujib-ur-Rahman

Recently, I got a chance to read the autobiography of Sheikh Mujib-ur-Rahman. Although it was incomplete, it had all the events that he experienced till the year 1955, all of which had been

---

* Mukti Bahini was a guerrilla force created by Sheikh Mujib-ur-Rahman to fight against the atrocities on the East Pakistani people by the West Pakistani armed forces.

penned by him while he was in jail. Later, after his unfortunate murder, this manuscript was handed over to his daughter Sheikh Hasina by one of his relatives. It is quite possible that he had written something more, but in 1971, the Pakistan Army raided his house situated in Dhanmondi (Dhaka, the capital city of Bangladesh) and confiscated all the documents present there; these could never be recovered and were lost in time. Out of love and deep attachment for her father, the pages of this incomplete autobiography were immaculately preserved by Sheikh Hasina just as someone would keep a priceless masterpiece, and she later had it published.

Written in Bengali, this biography describes in detail how Sheikh Mujib-ur-Rahman, being a member of the Muslim League, fought till the end for the creation of Pakistan and how the leaders of East Pakistan were mistreated by their counterparts in West Pakistan, because of which he resigned from the Muslim League and formed the Awami League. Even after the creation of Pakistan, the government in power tortured him to the extent that cannot be quantified in words; he had to spend most of his life behind bars. Finally, in the year 1971, Bangladesh came into existence, of which he served as prime minister till 1975. But later, he was overthrown by the army chief. He and his entire family, except two daughters, were murdered.

Since his two daughters, Sheikh Hasina and Sheikh Rehana, were residing abroad, they survived. Out of the two, Sheikh Hasina has been serving as the prime minister of Bangladesh for almost one and a half decades. So far fifty years have passed since the country's independence, but the memories of torture and mental agony reside in the minds of the Bangladeshis even today.

A few years ago, my wife Anuradha had interviewed General Pervez Musharraf, the former president of Pakistan, in Dubai for her channel News 24. I was also present during the interview. Somewhere in the middle, it turned into a heated discussion when my wife asked Musharraf, 'Why is Pakistan sponsoring terrorism in Kashmir?' After being continuously bombarded by such questions, Musharraf became agitated and countered, 'You are constantly talking about Pakistan's interference in Kashmir, but not even once have you talked about how India played its role in breaking Pakistan into two parts. The role of Indira Gandhi in the creation of Bangladesh out of East Pakistan has not been mentioned. It seems that you forgot this act of injustice by the leaders of your country but the people of Pakistan will never forget it. Moreover, I am an officer of the Pakistan Army, I will never forget the way our Indian counterparts made us surrender before them.' On that note, he finished what he had to say. He was so upset that the interview could not be resumed.

I still remember those words of Musharraf sahib. I decided to go back through history and start sifting across the relevant documents on the matter. Needless to say, Indira Gandhi did play a significant role in the creation of Bangladesh; however, the real culprits were different. The leaders of West Pakistan framed many conspiracies against the Bengali Muslims from day one. East Pakistanis were denied fundamental rights and instead were tortured to the extent that the separation of East Pakistan became almost inevitable.

All of these facts came into the limelight while I was reading the autobiography of Sheikh Mujib-ur-Rahman. As mentioned earlier, Sheikh Mujib was a disciple of Suhrawardy. He was a student leader whose passion and tenacity convinced Suhrawardy of his determination, and the senior leader handheld Sheikh Mujib to help him grow in his career. Sheikh Mujib had written that though Jinnah used to admire Suhrawardy a lot, various leaders of West Pakistan, such as Liaquat Ali Khan, had conspired against him. Iftikhar Hussain Khan Mamdot (Nawab of Mamdot; Mamdot was a princely state in the Punjab region of British India), who hailed from Eastern Punjab, became the chief minister of the Western Punjab province in Pakistan. On the other hand, Liaquat Ali Khan, who was a resident of the Indian state of Uttar

Pradesh, became the prime minister of Pakistan. But the whole game changed when it was time to appoint the prime minister of East Pakistan.

Suhrawardy was the sitting chief minister of East Pakistan, but he was told to contest elections if he wished to govern East Pakistan and that the MLAs would cast votes. When the elections came around, Prime Minister Liaquat Ali Khan and Union Minister Fazlur Rahman helped Khwaja Nazimuddin against Suhrawardy as a result of which Suhrawardy, who was the actual leader of Bengal, fell prey to their act of dishonesty and injustice.

After the Partition of 1947 when East and West Pakistan came to being, Nazimuddin was sworn in as the prime minister of East Pakistan, which was when the claim for Calcutta to be included in Pakistan was given up. According to Mujib-ur-Rahman, it was a conspiracy framed well in advance by Liaquat Ali and some other leaders of West Pakistan. The reason why they all gave up their claim over Calcutta was that if had become a part of Pakistan, then being the largest city, it would have been declared as the capital of East and West Pakistan; but they were all in favour of Karachi to be the capital as powers would remain in West Pakistan.

Mujib-ur-Rahman has written that the leaders of the Muslim League of Bengal, from the very beginning, had raised the demand for the inclusion of all of Bengal and Assam as a part of Pakistan; but since the Congress leaders of India were hand in glove with Viceroy Mountbatten and Radcliff, things didn't go well for them and finally, half of Bengal became a part of Pakistan and Assam was completely excluded. The West Pakistan leaders didn't want East Pakistan to be a large territory as it would have added to their problems.

The parliament of Pakistan would have been dominated by the members from East Pakistan and thus, important positions like that of the prime minister would have gone into the hands of the East Pakistanis. According to Mujib, it was a mistake on the part of Jinnah to be governor-general himself instead of offering that post to Mountbatten, which India did. He should have become the prime minister or president and let Mountbatten be the governor-general. Jawaharlal Nehru made this decision for India, because of which Mountbatten favoured India during the Partition.

Mujib has written that the central leadership of West Pakistan was so hostile to East Pakistani leaders that they dissolved their Bengal unit since a majority of its people supported Suhrawardy. The true leader of Bengal was ignored to such an extent that Suhrawardy finally decided to create his own party, which stood against the Muslim League, and the prominent leaders of which included Maulana Bhasani and Yar Mohammad Khan. Later, Suhrawardy decided that since they were secular people, they would omit 'Muslim' from the party name and rename it Awami League.

Sheikh Mujib has written that his first fight with West Pakistani authorities was regarding the inclusion of Bangla as an official language. Earlier it had been decided that if Urdu was made the national language of Pakistan, then the status of second official language would be given to Bangla. But the leaders of West Pakistan did not let that happen. As a consequence, the student division of the Awami League and later the Awami League itself started a movement for the recognition of the Bangla language which gained massive support. The leaders of the Awami League, even though they were Pakistani themselves, were being perceived as foes of their own country's government. They were thrown behind bars and were spied upon by secret police agencies. Sheikh Mujib wrote that though the country became independent, people were finding it hard to put an end to their problems and struggles. The country was going through a phase where people were suffering due to a famine, political workers were being sent to jail without proper trials and the leaders of the Muslim League were reluctant to recognize Bangla as the second national language. While West Pakistan saw rapid growth due to industrialization, East Pakistan was facing stagnancy. Sheikh Mujib wrote, 'I was once beaten blue and black by the police in Dhaka, I became unconscious and fell into the gutter.'

He has written, 'The prime minister of Pakistan, Liaquat Ali, in one of the meetings of the League, announced that they will kill the followers and supporters of Awami League.' Liaquat Ali Khan's objective was to ensure that no other party except the Muslim League existed in Pakistan. He probably forgot that he was the prime minister of the whole country and not just the Muslim League. In one of the public meetings of the Muslim League, he made an announcement that whoever supported the Awami League would have their heads crushed.

His style of governing resembled the traits of a dictator rather than a democratic leader's. After the demise of Jinnah, he started torturing his opponents, sent them to jail and stood completely against East Pakistan. Moreover, in one of his speeches in Karachi, he referred to Suhrawardy as the 'Dog of India'.

According to Mujib, Liaquat Ali did not make any significant contribution towards the movement for the creation of Pakistan. He was only a close aide of Jinnah and used to give eloquent speeches in Delhi. Had the students of Aligarh Muslim University not gone to help Liaquat Ali win the elections, Rafi Ahmad Kidwai would have most likely defeated him. Suhrawardy made every possible effort to cooperate with the Muslim League, but Liaquat Ali conspired against him and ruined his efforts. Liaquat Ali wanted to create differences between the Punjabis and the Bengalis. He himself was a refugee who hailed from Uttar Pradesh, but he deceived the people of Bengal. They were neither considered for jobs in government offices and the military nor were they supported in trade/business. Situations and circumstances were created in such a way that the Muslims from West Pakistan and the Bengali Muslims were instigated against each other, which resulted in massive riots in which mostly Bengalis were killed.

These events described by Sheikh Mujib date back to 1955. After Liaquat Ali Khan, the subsequent leaders of Pakistan such as President Ayub Khan and Yahya Khan did not miss an opportunity to suppress the Bengali people of East Pakistan. The army killed thousands of people and raped the women. Consequently, refugees fleeing from East Pakistan entered India. It was then that Indira Gandhi intervened and raised this matter at the global level. Finally, a war erupted in 1971 between India and Pakistan and a separate country, Bangladesh, came into being.

All this to say that Musharraf sahab may well say what he wants but the fact remains that the real culprits behind the creation of Bangladesh were none other than the leaders of West Pakistan. Indira Gandhi's intervention was an event that occurred much later, when East Pakistani refugees had started streaming into India. Had Musharraf sahab gone through the autobiography of Sheikh Mujib, he may not have lost his temper during the interview.

12

Manmohan Singh

The Saviour of the Indian Economy
Who Hailed from Pakistan

This is the story of one of India's prime ministers, who held the top post for ten long years. He had also served earlier as the finance minister of the country and the governor of the Reserve Bank of India. He was the head of the Planning Commission of India and served as the governor of the International Monetary Fund. It is hard to imagine that a person who has such important positions in the government and played a key role in shaping the future of India used to work at his father's grocery store in 1948 when he was about sixteen years old. This store was situated in an area known as Majith Mandi in Amritsar, Punjab. If it were not for his sheer determination and hard work, he would have continued to work at his father's grocery store and probably would have lived an ordinary life, but his destiny was to serve as the topmost official of the country.

He initially wanted to become a doctor but because of his disinterest in the essential subjects, he started studying at Hindu

College in Amritsar, from where he completed his BA (Honours) in economics. Before this, he had completed his intermediate college degree from Khalsa Inter College. Following his graduation, he took admission in Hoshiarpur Government College, Panjab University, to pursue an MA in economics.

We are talking about Manmohan Singh. He was born on 26 September 1932 in Gah village of Jhelum district (part of present-day Pakistan). In those days, keeping official birth records was not a common practice. Hence, some people refer to 4 February 1932 as his date of birth too. But the widely recognized date is 26 September. Manmohan's village had a school, but that was only up to class 4. So, for further studies, like everyone from his village, he had to go to a nearby settlement called Chakwal.

He was admitted to his village school in 1937 as per the records there and his date of birth is recorded as February 1932. At that time he was addressed as Mohan. His father's name was Gurmukh Singh Kohli and mother's name was Amrita Kaur. His mother succumbed to typhoid when he was very young and Mohan had no memories of her. He was brought up and looked after by his grandparents. His best friends at school were his classmates Gulam Mohammad Shah Wali Khan and Mohammad Ashraf. These days the village of Gah comes under Chakwal district. Although it has been now been declared a district, at the time of his birth, Chakwal fell under the Jhelum district. Notably, two of independent India's prime ministers, Inder Kumar Gujral and Manmohan Singh, were from the Jhelum district of undivided India.

Manmohan's father used to work as a clerk in a private company that was in the business of trading dry fruits. He started staying with his father in Peshawar after completing his studies till class 5 in Chakwal. Until 1947, he was studying at Khalsa Boys School in Peshawar in undivided India (part of Pakistan now). The standard of the education at the school was high and co-curricular activities were also encouraged at the school. Here, he exercised daily, which turned into a lifelong habit. The school library was filled with books on various subjects and students were encouraged to read. Manmohan had a knack for reading and read many books, including those on history and Urdu literature in Gurumukhi and English. He was a bright boy. He topped his school and stood third in the province for the class 8 exams conducted in the year 1945. This established him as a meritorious and promising student and teachers made sure that he got all the help he needed to do even better.

The year 1947 was Manmohan's final year in school. The matriculation exam took place in March. The communal tension during this time was getting worse every day because of the impending partition of the country. He sat for his exams in an environment filled with harrowing sights of violence; the results were never announced for the exams as Peshawar went on to become a part of Pakistan. Manmohan took the matriculation exams again when they were conducted in Delhi in 1948 for those who wanted to appear for it. He travelled from Haldwani (where he had moved with his family) to take the exam and again proved his mettle by scoring very well, despite having experienced the recent horrors of Partition.

The Four-Word Telegram

In 1947, the Hindu–Muslim clashes had begun, and they became more and more violent with each passing day. At his village, Muslims outnumbered all others and as a result, the village had two masjids and one gurudwara. One day, when the tension between the communities was at its peak, it was decided by the elders of the village that they would sit with each other and try to diffuse the tension with discussions. The elders of the village, who were Hindu, Sikh and Muslim, were called. However, the youngsters of the dominant Muslim community planned a massacre and killed all the Hindu and Sikh elders, among whom was Manmohan

Singh's grandfather, who had brought up young Manmohan and
of whom Manmohan was very fond. When his grandfather was
killed, Manmohan was living with his father in Peshawar. One
of his uncles who lived in Chakwal sent an unfortunate four-
word telegram to his brother (Manmohan's father) in Peshawar
that read, 'Mother Safe, Father Killed'. Manmohan was about
fifteen years old at the time and says that he still remembers that
dreadful telegram message.* He says that on the one hand, this
group of young Muslim men tricked and killed his grandfather
and on the other hand, in that very neighbourhood, there was a
Muslim family who hid his grandmother and protected her from
the bloodthirsty mob.

These incidents from his childhood were so deeply etched
in his memory that while working for the United Nations
Conference on Trade and Development in the United States
of America, when he was invited by his friend to Pakistan, he
could not resist visiting. His friend Mahbub-ul-Haq had studied
with him at Cambridge University in the United Kingdom. He
later served as the finance minister of Pakistan. Mahbub used to
stay in Rawalpindi, Pakistan, in those days. It was in 1968 that
Manmohan Singh visited Pakistan. After the Indo-Pak War of
1965, the relations between the two countries was at its lowest, but
Manmohan could not say no to the invitation extended by his very
dear friend and visited Rawalpindi, a place he used to visit often
in his schooldays. There, he used to visit a particular bookshop,
and during this trip, it was in the same shop that he found himself
gripped by all the nostalgia from his childhood.

After that, he visited Gurudwara Panja Sahib situated in
Hassan Abdal (Attock in Punjab, Pakistan) where his naming
ceremony had taken place. When he was asked why he did not
visit his birthplace, Gah village, which was nearby, his answer

---

* Daman Singh, *Strictly Personal: Manmohan and Gursharan*, Harper
Collins India (Kindle Edition), 2014, p. 28.

expressed the sadness that he had been carrying in his heart for years. He said that he did not visit his village because he did not want to inflict on himself the emotional trauma of going to the place where his grandfather had been massacred brutally. During the peak of the violence that had erupted there at the time of Partition, all the houses were burned to the ground; so Manmohan was unsure if there even was anything left to see. His uncle who used to live in Chakwal till 1947 had visited Gah village with a police contingent and had taken the remaining Sikh and Hindu women safely to Chakwal, where they were accommodated in a refugee camp. Manmohan said that not all the women could be saved from the horrendous riots; his own aunt and her mother chose self-immolation to save themselves from being violated by the mobs.*

When I was a minister in the Planning Commission, I worked very closely with Manmohan Singh, who was the head of the Planning Commission by virtue of being the prime minister of the country. After one of my visits to Pakistan, I was telling him about my trip to Gurudwara Nankana Sahib and how the managing committee members of the gurudwara were complaining about the fact that they were not issued visas to India as they were citizens of Pakistan; they had requested me to convey this problem to Manmohan Singh. It was during this discussion that he expressed a wish to visit Pakistan as the prime minister of India, but unfortunately did not think it would be possible. When I enquired about where he wished to go, he said he wanted to visit his village this time and see his school. I told him he should certainly go. I could sense the sea of emotions in his moist eyes and in his voice. Unfortunately, he could never visit Pakistan as the prime minister of the country as he had to step down from his post in 2014.

---

* Singh, *Strictly Personal.*

From Grocery Store to Cambridge

In 1947, when his grandfather was murdered, his father was still working in Peshawar. During the months of May and June when the environment for non-Muslims was getting worse, Manmohan's father decided to bring all his children to his friend's house in Haldwani in Uttar Pradesh, India, via train. Singh says that at the age of fourteen, he felt excited as it was his first long train journey. During this long ride, the train passed through Lahore, Amritsar, Saharanpur and Bareilly, among many other cities, before it reached Haldwani. He said city life was new for him compared to the way he used to live before. His family had brought along some bedding and a few clothes to this new city to start their life over again. Initially, he thought that they were going to Haldwani for a few days and once the conditions got better, they would return to their home in Peshawar.

Before coming to Haldwani, Manmohan's father had left his job at the private firm and set up his own small business in Peshawar. To take care of the business, his father had to go back to Peshawar once he had made sure that his children were safe with his friend in Haldwani. December 1947 was very stressful for fifteen-year-old Manmohan, who knew nothing about the whereabouts of his father and could not establish any contact with him for days at a stretch as there were no telephones in those days. He would go to the Haldwani railway station every day to see if his father had arrived in any one of the trains.

In the meanwhile, the communal situation had deteriorated even further; his father had to close his business in Peshawar and had to cross over to independent India from the Wagah border. As after leaving his entire business in Peshawar he had nothing to do there, he decided to settle down in the city of Amritsar and opened a grocery store at the Majith Mandi area while staying in a nearby area known as Kanak Mandi in the city.

Manmohan told his daughter in a conversation, which she included in her book, 'We didn't have differences, but I didn't like sitting in the shop. I felt that due respect was not given to me.' Manmohan's father did not treat him well and used to give him menial jobs, due to which Manmohan got very sad, and returned to his studies.* He got enrolled in Hindu College in September 1948. Since the family was yet to find its feet financially, Manmohan joined Hindu College as he could go there on foot since it was a twenty-five-minute walk; Khalsa College was far away and he could not afford the hostel fees. He chose humanities with economics, political science, mathematics, English and French. In the year 1950, he topped the university examinations, which won him a two-year scholarship at the college.

Manmohan was deeply interested in economics. The reason why some countries were rich and others poor intrigued him as a student, and it was this curiosity that put him on the path to becoming a world-renowned economist who occupied many important positions related to economic policy nationally and internationally.

It was in the year 1952 that he finally got a chance to move out of his home by securing the first position in his graduation examination and got a chance to study further at the Hoshiarpur College on a scholarship offered by the Panjab University. Unlike two years ago, his father could now afford his hostel fees and Manmohan moved 110 kilometres from home to the city of Hoshiarpur in Punjab, India.

His economics theory teacher, Rangnekar, encouraged Manmohan Singh to apply for a scholarship to the University of Cambridge to continue his studies as he foresaw a bright academic future for him. Cambridge University was the mecca of economics, which would give the required global exposure to the very bright Manmohan Singh. While awaiting word on his

* Singh, *Strictly Personal,* p. 58.

acceptance at Cambridge, he started his research scholarship at Panjab College. He got a lot of support from everyone for the detailed documentation that was required to go to the United Kingdom; his vice chancellor let him keep his research scholarship, which assisted his stay at St John's College in Cambridge where he got accepted. Manmohan left for the United Kingdom by ship in September 1955.

While Cambridge was a big shift for this boy who was born in a village, he adapted quickly. This could be attributed to the experience of Partition that had made him more resilient, a trait which everyone who went through the horrors of the dreadful events of 1947 seemed to have acquired. The only problem that bothered this young boy was a lack of money. He planned all the expenses that he would incur over the next two years of his stay in the United Kingdom and the calculations came to a sum of £600. He had about £160 from his Panjab University scholarship and for the rest, he was dependent on his father. He decided to live frugally because he did not want to bother his father much. He seldom ate out and used to eat at the college dining hall, where the food was relatively cheap at two shillings and six pence. Still, he would sometimes be in a tight spot when he fell short of money; but he did always get it from home, even if the money arrived late. In those conditions, he would skip meals and lived on Cadbury's chocolate bars that would cost six pence. He chose not to borrow money from anyone in college, a habit he retained and never borrowed from anyone in his life. The only person he requested for assistance when things got very bad was his friend Madan Lal Sudan, whom he knew from his postgraduation days in Hoshiarpur College. He wrote him a letter stating he might fall £25 pounds short over the course of the next two years of his stay in the UK, and he therefore hoped that his friend could send him £12 that year and £13 next year. Two months later, a money order for £3 came for him; this was probably all that his dear friend could afford to send to him, and Manmohan was forever grateful to his friend for the gesture.

At the end of the first year of college, when the results for the examinations were declared, it was found that Manmohan had aced them. He wrote to his friend Madan that he must not send him any more money as he would be getting a prize worth £20, which would take care of the anticipated shortfall in the budget.

In the year 1991, when Manmohan Singh was appointed the twenty-second finance minister of India and presented the landmark budget in the Parliament, he was hailed as the economist who averted a major financial crisis in the country, as India was left with only two weeks' import worth of foreign exchange reserves. It was then that he suggested deregulation of the Indian economy for inflow of foreign investments into the country. It is widely perceived that Manmohan Singh was spotted as the candidate for the post of finance minister by the former prime minister P.V. Narsimha Rao. But I would like to state here that it was Sonia Gandhi who suggested his name and assigned Manmohan Singh the responsibility of managing the finance portfolio in the government as she had seen up-close his work on various fiscal and economic matters during Indira Gandhi and Rajiv Gandhi's governments.

This boy from a small village achieved great things with his intelligence, grit and resilience. But his tryst with Partition took away his beloved grandfather and he was never able to fulfil his dream of visiting his first home one last time as the prime minister of India.

References

Akbar, M.J. *Gandhi's Hinduism: The Struggle against Jinnah's Islam.* Bloomsbury, 2000.

Gujral, I.K. *Matters of Discretion: An Autobiography.* Hay House, 2017.

Gujral, Satish. A Brush with Life: An Autobiography. Viking, 1997.

Lapierre Dominique and Larry Collins. *Freedom at Midnight.* Simon & Schuster, 1975.

Malik, Hafeez, ed. *Pakistan: Founder's Aspirations and Today's Realities.* Oxford University Press, 2001.

Rahman, Sheikh Mujbir. *The Unfinished Memoirs.* Penguin Books, India, 2012.

Salim, Ahmad. *Lahore 1947.* Tara-India Research Press, 2001.

Singh, Daman. *Strictly Personal: Manmohan and Gursharan.* Harper Collins India, 2014.

Acknowledgements

I first visited Pakistan in 1988 as a journalist in the Indian delegation led by Prime Minister Rajiv Gandhi during the SAARC summit. It was this trip that put me on a path that led to this book. My first observation upon meeting the people of Pakistan was that they are in no way different from Indians. This sparked the desire to meet and interact with more people who were affected during the Partition from both sides of the border and share their stories with the world.

I would like to acknowledge some people from both Indian and Pakistan who have motivated me and helped this book see the light of the day.

From India, I.K. Gujral, former prime minister of India, and Kuldip Nayar, eminent journalist. Parliamentarian and former Indian High Commissioner to the UK Rajinder Sachar, who served as the chief justice of Delhi High Court and was the one person who always checked on the progress of the book, even when it was just an idea; the question he posed remained with me all these years and I had to answer it with this book. Naresh Gujral helped me with many relevant facts and photographs for this book. M.J. Akbar, Indian journalist and parliamentarian, also encouraged me.

From Pakistan, Shahryar Khan, former foreign secretary and former chairman of the Pakistan Cricket Board along with his wife Minoo Khan; Chaudhary Shujat Hussain, former prime minister of Pakistan; and Salman Siddique, former finance secretary of Pakistan are some of the people who always inquired after the progress of this book in most of our encounters, be it professional or personal.

My special thanks to Priyanka Gandhi, who gave the idea to Meru Gokhale, publisher, Penguin Random House India, to publish this book and to Meru for making it available to readers worldwide.

My wife, Anurradha (editor-in-chief, News 24), and daughter, Vaanya, were the people who constantly gave me constructive feedback on the book. From my staff, Alok Srivastava, Mohammad Akram, Mukesh Arora and Puneet Dutta helped me gather and put together the content and images for the book. Anant Bajaj contributed in the translation of the book and Ankit Chatterjee assisted me in editing it.